U-BOAT KILLER

U-BOAT KILLER

FIGHTING THE U-BOATS IN THE
BATTLE OF THE ATLANTIC

CAPTAIN
DONALD MACINTYRE

CASSELL&CO

Cassell Military Paperbacks

Cassell & Co
Wellington House, 125 Strand
London WC2R 0BB

Copyright © Donald Macintyre 1956

First published by Weidenfeld & Nicolson 1956
This Cassell Military Paperbacks edition 1999
Reprinted 2000, 2002

British Library Cataloguing-in-Publication Data
A catalogue record for this book is available from the British Library

ISBN 0-304-35235-7

Printed and bound by
The Guernsey Press, Guernsey, C.I.

CONTENTS

LIST OF ILLUSTRATIONS

Between pages 84-85

The Author

HMS *Hesperus* in her war paint

With her bows dangerously buckled the *Hesperus* returns to port after ramming and sinking *U 357*

Some of our prisoners come ashore

The *Hesperus's* crew kept the score of U-boats sunk

Two of the drawings by Commander 'Jackie' Broome which enlivened the official Convoy Instructions

Distribution map of British shipping in Home Waters, Atlantic and Mediterranean on an average day before introduction of convoys

Distribution map of British and American convoys and ships sailing independently in Home Waters, Atlantic and Mediterranean in mid-August 1943

The Author and his First-Lieutenant, Commander Ridley, on the bridge of the *Bickerton*

The end of HMS *Bickerton*

The photographs are reproduced by kind permission of the Imperial War Museum

FOREWORD

by Admiral Robert B. Carney

CAPTAIN Donald Macintyre, RN, here tells a saga of destroyers and the men who man them. With a modesty and conciseness which, if anything, add to the vividness of his story, Captain Macintyre takes his readers through moments of high adventure, periods of devastating boredom, and the utter misery that can only come to sailors in small ships in the wretched North Atlantic. Through his eyes we glimpse the stunning savagery of the battle for the Empire's lifeline. It is an intensely human story, devoid of melodramatic embellishment, but it also points up the stark need for effective sea power in an era in which it is difficult to retain a sense of perspective in the face of the dramatic developments in the field of mass-destruction weapons.

And yet, in spite of the deep underlying seriousness of Captain Macintyre's account, one can discern the ever-present Scottish twinkle which made him a delightful and never-to-be-forgotten companion.

Captain Macintyre has not only written an intensely interesting and human story; he also makes one aware of the value of stamina and character. He teaches a military lesson for the tactician and the leader; but there is an even greater lesson underlying his account of the grim struggle which finally brought the German submarine service to its knees and saved a valiant Britain in a dark and desperate hour. If the Allies had lost control of the sea to Hitler's Navy, all Britain's valour and resolution would have been to no avail, for she could not have continued the battle on to victory without the flow of lifeblood across the Atlantic.

What was true in those days—and in other well-remembered days along the Atlantic sea lanes in World War I—is just as true to-day, and possibly even more significant. The perennial submarine menace is still a vital factor in every consideration of national and Western security. Considering the vastly greater number of submarines available to the USSR to-day, in comparison with what Hitler had to work with, the gravity of the situation cannot be disregarded. Unfortunately, the spectacular developments in the field of mass-destruction weapons have given rise to fears and concerns which have, at times, eclipsed serious consideration of other important factors. It has been claimed that aerial atomic warfare would be so swift and so cataclysmic that all would be over in a matter of weeks, or days, or hours; in such a situation, many ask, 'Why bother with Navies at all? And yet the philosophy which prompts such thinking loses sight of many realities. Suppose, for example, that a brave nation refused to surrender even in the face of such an aerial holocaust; how, then, could it carry on? Certainly, continuation of the struggle would be impossible if the sea lanes were denied to us. Suppose, for example again, that diplomacy and reason—or other political considerations—led to written or tacit agreement for the limitation of atomic warfare; then if the Western alliance were beguiled into abdicating its position at sea, its ultimate security would be just as surely doomed.

The sea still remains a vital battlefield and we must retain our position of pre-eminence on the oceans just as surely as we must be equipped to meet the new threat from the skies.

Perhaps the Epilogue is the most significant part of Captain Macintyre's book, for there, with his simple but eloquent turn of phrase, he brings home the vital need to retain our mastery of the sea lanes necessary for our security and our survival.

In addition to the importance of a convoy system, as emphasized by Captain Macintyre, there are certain other factors which must now be considered. In the decade since the close of hostilities in 1945, many things have happened, many inventions have been incorporated into military techniques, and new horizons have been opened in both strategy and tactics. To-day, it is the considered opinion of the United States Navy that the submarine must be attacked at its bases and in its own home waters, it must be sought out, intercepted and attacked *en route* to and from its patrol areas. It is not sufficient merely to be prepared to meet it should it win through to a firing position close to our precious convoys. The submarine menace itself has increased in significance, but, by the same token, the menace to the submarine has increased with the acquisition of new weapons and the introduction of new techniques. We must be prepared with these greater capabilities to suppress the greater menace.

Captain Macintyre has rendered a public service with his fine story and he has endeared himself to destroyer sailors the world over. My own affection for him is the greater because his clear and authentic prose made me live again, for an hour or two, my own wonderful days as a destroyer sailor.

ROBERT B. CARNEY, ADMIRAL
UNITED STATES NAVY (Retired)

PREFACE

WHEN a friend suggested to me that I should make a book of my experiences in the Battle of the Atlantic, I at first rejected the idea. I felt that a truthful account of the largely humdrum doings of an Escort Force Commander would seem a dull and pedestrian affair to those who have enjoyed the highly dramatic and very successful novels on the war at sea which have already been published. As I thought it over, however, and particularly when I tried to read myself the latest of these best sellers and discovered it to be the most appalling farago of nonsense, presenting a wildly distorted view of wartime life in the Royal Navy, I came to the conclusion that perhaps, after all, there was need for a factual account of the war against the U-boats as seen by one who took part in it from the beginning until nearly the end.

This book inevitably consists for the most part of accounts of the more exciting moments of my three and a half years in the Western Approaches Command. I was fortunate in having rather more than my share of such moments and that, in spite of mistakes on my part, they were mostly attended by success. But they must be viewed against the background of many voyages devoid of incidents worth recounting. For long periods the Battle of the Atlantic would consist of slow and wearisome voyages in tempestuous weather, yet made utterly rewarding by the sight of the fleets of deeply-laden freighters and tankers safely brought to harbour with the supplies without which the war could not have been waged.

Finally I would like to stress that Naval successes are almost invariably the result of team-work and training; that failure by the humblest member of the team can ruin the efforts of all. This book is therefore my tribute to all those who sailed with me and suffered the discomforts, amounting often to misery, of life in a small ship on the Atlantic run, but stayed cheerful and steady through it all so that, when the infrequent occasions of combat arose, they were ready and alert to play their part. Very few of them could be rewarded with decorations to commemorate their gallant service and I hope this account of the actions which we shared may to some degree compensate them.

I wish to acknowledge the assistance given me by the Historical Section of the Admiralty, where I received much ungrudging aid in my researches from Mr G. H. Hurford, F.R.Hist.S., and his busy staff.

From Commander F. Barley RNVR of the same section I received a great deal of helpful comment and guidance as well as the benefit of his unparalleled knowledge of the defence of our Merchant shipping in two World Wars.

To the officers in charge of Records at the Admiralty, under Mr Ellmers, I owe an immense debt for the willing assistance given me in resurrecting my old Reports of Proceedings from their graves in the Archives. Without them the fallibility of the human memory would often have led me astray.

The two drawings facing page 60 are the work of Captain J. E. Broome, DSC, RN, and were originally illustrations which helped to enliven the otherwise arid pages of the Western Approaches Convoy Instructions. I am grateful for his permission to reproduce them here and to the RNVR Club, who kindly lent the originals for that purpose.

To Terence Robertson, author of *The Golden Horseshoe*, an account of the career of the German U-Boat Ace, Otto Kretschmer, I owe the inspiration and encouragement to write my own story.

Finally I must record how pleased I am that my old friend, Admiral Robert B. Carney, until recently Chief of Naval Operations of the US Navy, has done me the honour of writing the foreword. His opinions are worthy of the highest respect. His kind judgment of my efforts I shall always cherish.

D.M.

CHAPTER 1

The First Months of War

THE spring of 1939, with the war clouds gathering over Europe, found me enjoying foreign service leave after returning from a two-year commission in command of the destroyer *Defender* on the China Station.

The thirteen years of service that had passed since I had been commissioned as Sub-Lieutenant had been divided almost equally between destroyers and the Fleet Air Arm, two branches of the Navy that were ideally suited to give me the training necessary for the role that I was destined to fill in the war that was coming. On first being commissioned I had found myself appointed to a destroyer in the Mediterranean, then, as now, the chief training ground of our fleet. Under captains who were veteran destroyer officers of the First World War, I experienced the thrill of ship-handling at high-speed close formation manœuvres in which only a trained 'seaman's eye' and split-second thinking could ensure safety, let alone the perfection that was demanded. We constantly practised night actions and night scouting and I learnt the technique of being able to distinguish in the blackness the darker shape which was another ship, and to estimate its course and speed from the faint white gleams of bow wave and wake.

All this was to stand me in good stead later. But soon after I was promoted to Lieutenant in 1926, came a different call which I could not resist. The Fleet Air Arm, which since the absorption in 1918 of the RNAS in the newly-formed Royal Air Force had been manned by the RAF, was by then 'navalised' to the extent that half the pilots and all the observers were naval officers. I volunteered as a pilot and was soon on my way home to the start of seven very happy and rewarding years of naval flying.

Our flying training in those days was entirely in the hands of the RAF, so that for the next year my life was spent at RAF stations at Netheravon on Salisbury Plain, Leuchars in Fife, and Lee-on-Solent. In order that we might be legally subject to and in turn able to enforce the RAF Discipline Act, naval pilots were given, in addition to their naval commissions, commissions as Flying Officers RAF. This created some strange anomalies as one's RAF rank did not increase with one's naval promotion and cases arose in which a Lieut.-Commander or even a Commander RN, being still a Flying Officer RAF, found himself when ashore liable for subordinate duties and under the command of Flight-Lieutenants many years his juniors. With sensible give-and-take such difficulties ironed themselves out, but at times they certainly gave rise to ill-feeling.

I enjoyed every minute of the training which naturally culminated in the great day when one first landed on the deck of a carrier. I still remember vividly the feeling of dismay and alarm with which I watched the first of my batch of initiates go straight over the side of the *Furious* into the sea. All went well, however, when my own turn came and by the end of the day I was a fully-fledged Fleet Air Arm fighter pilot.

The years that followed in the *Hermes* on the China station and the *Courageous* at home were from a personal point of view entirely fascinating and rewarding. The immense potential importance of the air to naval warfare made everything we did exciting. But at the same time we chafed at the appalling lack of appreciation of what aircraft could do. Gunnery was the naval officer's god, as it had been since before the age of steam, and ex-gunnery officers occupied most of the positions on the Flag List at that time. Professional pride scorned any suggestion that the pathetic anti-aircraft armament of those days could not cope with air attack. As a consequence money which might have gone to building up the Fleet Air Arm was diverted to the building and upkeep of battleships, some of which barely fired a shot in anger during the war.

In the years to come the Navy was to cry in vain for the

carriers which should have been built and to see the latest battleship, the *Prince of Wales*, and the battle-cruiser *Repulse*, darlings of the gunnery branch, sunk at their first encounter with the scorned torpedo-bomber.

My time with the Fleet Air Arm came to an end when a serious illness in 1935 left me temporarily unfit for flying. To my joy, when I was passed fit for sea service again, a lucky break gained me an appointment in command. The first of a new class of anti-submarine ships, the *Kingfisher*, was under construction at Fairfield's yard on the Clyde. I stood by her final fitting-out and watched her maker's trials. At last came the day when I ordered her White Ensign and commissioning pennant to be hoisted and found myself at that supreme moment of a naval officer's life—in command of my first ship.

Seven years of flying had left my navigational knowledge with a thick coating of rust and it was with some trepidation that I set off for my home port in a south-westerly gale. I had to relearn fast in order to keep out of trouble and, in later months when experience had freshened my memory of the age-old nautical rules for the safe conduct of a ship at sea, I looked back with horror at some of the unprofessional methods I had managed to get away with by good fortune.

It was in *Kingfisher* that I first acquired my overriding interest in submarine hunting, for she became the experimental ship for the Anti-Submarine School at Portland. There she received any and every new gadget that was devised, and many a long and fascinating day I spent trying them out in company with that devoted godfather of the asdic, Professor Jock Anderson. I often wonder whether the Navy in general appreciates what it owes to that indefatigable man who nursed the asdic from its unsatisfactory infancy to its splendid maturity as a war-winning instrument. His enthusiasm knew no bounds. Invariably dreadfully seasick, nothing daunted Jock Anderson and, with his personal bucket ever at hand, he was always present to test his theories and devices in person.

The asdic in its first primitive form was devised towards

the end of the First World War. Its basic principles have remained unchanged but with the passing years its efficiency and scope and the means of applying it to deliver an attack on the submarine have all steadily advanced. Basically it consists of a transmitter-receiver which sends out impulses of a sound wave on any selected bearing and picks up the same impulses should they strike an object and be reflected. These transmissions and their echoes are made audible, through earphones or loudspeakers, as a musical note best described as 'Ping'. Hence the asdic was known as the 'Ping set', operating the asdic was known as 'Pinging' and the anti-submarine specialist officer as a 'Pinger'. By mounting the transmitter-receiver so that it can be trained round like a submarine searchlight, the direction in which the 'ping' goes out (and consequently the direction in which lies the object from which the 'ping' is reflected) can be read off from a compass receiver. By noting the interval of time between the transmission and the return of its 'echo', the range of the object can be obtained.

So far the theory is quite simple, but in practice a number of circumstances arise to complicate the picture. The transmitter-receiver must obviously be below the surface of the water, and immersed in the water, and being by its nature a form of hydrophone, as the ship moves through the water the noise of the water sweeping across it will drown the noise of the 'ping' unless steps are taken to avoid this. So the instrument is encased in a metal 'dome' projecting from the ship's bottom. The dome is filled with water and thus as the ship goes ahead the instrument remains immersed in sea-water but relatively stationary sea-water. But even so, only at moderate speeds could the noise level in the asdic be kept low enough for it to function. Therefore whenever a ship wished to operate its asdic to search for or hunt a submarine it had to moderate its speed.

Another characteristic of the instrument is that the sound beam sent out is conical in shape. The further an impulse goes from the transmitter the broader and deeper is the area it covers. Thus, though an object at a depth of, say, 500 feet would be in the beam at a range of 1,000 yards, as the range

4

lessens the object would become below the lower limit of the cone of sound and would thus cease to send back a reflection or echo. This characteristic had the advantage of allowing one to make a rough guess at the depth of a submarine, but it also had the great drawback that, when attacking with depth-charges, one had a long interval, out of contact with the target, before reaching the firing position. This was to give us considerable difficulty when the German U-boats took to diving to great depths when attacked and special attack methods had to be devolved to deal with the problem.

When searching with the asdic, the procedure was to sweep across a broad arc from one side of the ship's course to the other, stopping every few degrees to transmit a 'ping', listen for any echo coming back, and then to train the asdic round a few degrees and repeat the process. A fairly wide section of water was thus covered by each complete sweep. If several ships were searching together, they would be spread in a line abreast a mile or a mile and a half apart, so that the path swept by the asdic of one ship would be touching the path swept by the ships adjacent, leaving no water unswept between.

Should an echo be received, the sound beam would be held on to it, the range and bearing could be read off and passed to the plotting table and when a number of such ranges and bearings had been received, the plot operator could read the course and speed of the target. If it was moving at all it might be a U-boat, but as whales and shoals of fish also sent back an echo, this was by no means a certainty. Similarly, if stationary it was unlikely to be a submarine as a submarine generally requires some forward motion to allow its hydroplanes to help it keep at a set depth. On the other hand in shallow water the stationary echo might come from a 'bottomed' submarine.

Thus there were a number of modifications to the simple theoretical operation of the asdic. To an inexperienced operator all echoes were the same, submarines, fish, tide rips, rocks or even sheer imagination. The experienced U-boat hunter on the other hand developed a sort of sixth sense. The echo from a submarine was to him in some indefinable and unexplainable way different from any other. But no operator was infallible and always, when sweeping for submarines with the asdic, the decision whether to attack or ignore a contact had to be made. The number of depth-charges available and the desirability of conserving them for more positive contacts, the gap left in the screen if you dropped out to attack, the confusion and alarm that might be unnecessarily caused in the convoy if you gave your opinion that it was a submarine—all these factors had to be weighed before the decision could be taken.

Once it was decided to attack, the procedure was to point one's ship at the target and close it at a moderate speed. By the time the range was down to about 1,000 yards, sufficient data would have reached the plot to give a course and speed of the target. Course would then be altered so as to 'collide' with the submarine, and as the ship passed over it, or rather passed a little way ahead to allow for the time taken by depth-charges to sink, a pattern of depth charges would be fired. Those from the chutes in the stern would be dropped at evenly-spaced intervals in the wake, while the depth-charge throwers would send others out some fifty yards on either side. Thus the pattern properly laid would form a shape like an elongated diamond, somewhere inside of which, one hoped, would be the target. But to produce lethal damage the charges must explode near the U-boat in depth as well as in plan and as the depth of the submarine was largely a matter of guesswork the charges were fired at varying depths to increase the chance of success.

Such in brief outline was the asdic and the depth-charge attack as we knew them in the early days of the Atlantic battle. Of course, there were very many refinements of method and calculation. The effect of wind and weather on one's ship and consequently on the best direction from which to attack, the need to avoid presenting oneself as an easy target for a torpedo attack in retaliation, the ruses tried out to prevent the U-boat commander from knowing when one was making the final dash to drop depth charges—all were of vital importance to the U-boat hunter.

I was wonderfully lucky in the 'Ping' specialists who served with me in the two ships which I commanded for long periods of the war. In *Walker* the senior asdic rating, Backhouse, had the quiet confidence of the man who knows his job through and through. At the climax of a long night of confused fighting and mêlée, he was quite unperturbed and was able to classify the sounds in his headphones with the detachment acquired through long and wearisome practice. Later in *Hesperus* I had the incomparable Petty-Officer Coster, who could be relied on to hear the first faint echo from a submarine at the maximum range of the asdic. Teamed up with Bill Ridley, my First-Lieutenant and anti-submarine specialist officer, they were a deadly combination for any U-boat that came within *Hesperus* range.

In 1937 I graduated to my first destroyer, the *Defender*, on the China station. With her 35,000 HP and 32 knots, she was a very different proposition from my little 785-ton *Kingfisher* and her 20 knots. I thanked my stars for my early destroyer training in the old Mediterranean days as the flotilla streaked about the China Sea, performing its intricate manœuvres at 30 knots. But this soon came to an end with the beginning of the war between Japan and China, when every ship on the station was required to bring comfort and confidence to the many foreign communities in the ports up and down the China coast. 'Gunboat diplomacy' is out of fashion today, but in those days many a Western trader in China was very glad to see the White Ensign or the Stars and Stripes flying on a warship in the harbour.

The Munich crisis found *Defender* playing guardian angel to the foreign community of Amoy and the precarious position in which they would have found themselves in the event of war must have been brought home by our immediate departure for our war station at Singapore. But I was not to take *Defender* to war, and in the spring of 1939 I handed her over to my successor and sailed for home.

I hoped that when the buff envelope from the Admiralty arrived with my next appointment it would give me command of one of the new destroyers joining the fleet. It was not much cause for jubilation therefore when mobilisation of the Reserve Fleet was ordered and I was instructed to go to Rosyth to commission a destroyer veteran of the 1914–18 war, HMS *Venomous*. A destroyer is a destroyer though, I told myself resignedly, and set off. My gloom returned when I reached Rosyth and sought out from amongst the mass of ancient-looking V and W class destroyers lying in the dockyard basin the particular old warrior that had been selected for me.

I found that *Venomous* was a very dubious proposition. Built towards the end of the 1914-18 war, she had been equipped with an experimental machinery layout. For those of an engineering bent I will enlarge by saying that she was the first destroyer to be given a 'closed-feed system'. The system was experimental and had a number of defects; so, when the First World War came to an end, *Venomous* was hurriedly placed in reserve—and her engineers no doubt breathed a heavy sigh of relief.

In consequence I found that, unlike her sister ships, she had never been out of reserve since; that engineers, used either to more modern or more matured types of machinery, viewed her hybrid set with considerable alarm; and that none of the improvements by way of modernisation that had been given to others of her class had been given to her. This meant amongst other things that she had not been fitted with the asdic, the only device for detecting submerged submarines.

With her obsolete armament of 4-inch guns, no anti-submarine weapon and very doubtful machinery, she recalled the Duke of Wellington's scathing description of some troops under his command which 'might not frighten the enemy but, by God, they frighten me'.

However, we duly commissioned and a ship's company composed largely of experienced, time-expired reservists who 'knew the ropes' got things smoothly into shape. Smoke began to pour from the funnels, machinery came to reluctant life, giving the ship that vibration which is its soul, and in due time we nosed our way out into the Firth of Forth for trials and exercises.

These went off surprisingly well owing to my engineer officer's skilful manipulation of his strange machinery system, and we became part of the flotilla commanded by Captain Tom Halsey in the *Malcolm*. Our first assignment was to take part in the royal review of the Reserve Fleet in Weymouth Bay, the principal function of which was the presentation to His Majesty of all commanding officers and a selected number of officers and men from each ship. When my turn came I particularly noticed the glowering, surly face of Admiral Darlan, head of the French Navy, who had been invited to be present. At that time I had no idea that he had such an implacable hatred for the Royal Navy, but looking back it seems to me that he made no attempt on that occasion to hide his feelings. From Weymouth the flotilla went to its war station at Portsmouth and it was there that we heard Neville Chamberlain announce that we were at war with Germany.

The flotilla's function was to escort the ships carrying our troops across to France—and a very unrewarding task it turned out to be. Nightly, at around midnight, two or three ships of the flotilla would rendezvous, at the 'gate' of the boom which stretched across to the Isle of Wight, with the fast cross-Channel or Harwich packet boats which were employed as troopships. Having marshalled them into a body outside the boom, we would set off at a spanking 25 knots for Cherbourg or Le Havre where we would arrive at daylight. We usually had an hour or two to wait before bringing back an empty convoy and could sometimes get ashore for a brief shopping tour—Guerlain's perfume for our girl friends, and wine, were the only purchases I can remember. The former made us very popular ashore on our return and the latter soon gave *Venomous* a remarkably fine cellar for a modest price.

It was difficult to take our escorting duties very seriously for the enemy made no effort to interfere with these nightly runs. The chief difficulty I found was to cope with the rather hectic 'phoney war' conditions ashore (where I had just got to know the girl whom I later married), and then to take my ship out of harbour in the black-out and the rain and thread my way between the very dim lights marking the gate of the boom defences. With the fierce cross-tide at the gate it took some tricky manœuvring to wait while the troopships went through.

Once outside and round the Nab Tower this convoy of fast ships would hare slap across the main convoy route up the channel, showing no lights and of course without radar in those days. On at least one occasion we ran at right angles through a large convoy at 25 knots and it was a miracle that there were no collisions. It was all good practice for the problems of wartime navigation, which stood me in good stead later, but I felt a fraud in my old *Venomous*—our chief preoccupation was to keep up with our high-speed charges, let alone to protect them.

It was therefore with some excitement that I found the familiar official envelope containing a new appointment in my mail one morning early in January. Opening it I found that I was to command HMS *Hearty*, then in process of completion at Messrs Thorneycrofts shipyard at Woolston, near Southampton. The name of the ship meant little to me and it sounded more like a tugboat than anything, so it was a happy surprise when I found she was in fact a destroyer much like our own H class, though modified to suit the tastes of the Brazilians for whose navy she and five others were being built.

Turning *Venomous* over to my relief, John MacBeath, I hurried off to Thorneycrofts and there, lying at her buoys, I saw the ship that I knew I could lose my heart to. To try to explain this feeling would be as tedious as those passages of a novel in which the author describes the beauty of his heroine, so I will restrict myself to saying that she was a destroyer built on classical lines by Thorneycrofts, who are in my opinion the finest destroyer constructors in the world. But even the most attractive of heroines cannot be without flaw and *Hearty* had early faults to get over. These were chiefly due to her completion date being arbitrarily advanced by order of the Admiralty who were desperate to get ships to sea where there was a deadly shortage of craft to hunt the U-boats and escort our convoys. However, steam trials, gunnery trials and all the multifarious tests and calibrations required before formally commissioning went off well, and soon I had signed the receipt on behalf of the Admiralty for 'one destroyer'. We were ready for our first assignment: to test her out for teething troubles.

Owing to the hasty completion, we discovered that the steel plates of the upper deck had not been properly caulked, and the first time we found ourselves in a seaway, everyone between decks lived in a perpetual showerbath. Then we found that our gyro-compass, which was not the well-tried Sperry type that most warships had, was designed for the statelier motion of a merchant ship and when subjected to the lively antics of a destroyer threw in its hand in disgust, like a dignified dowager called upon to jive. The gunnery control system had been left incomplete and no director sight had been installed. Furthermore the instruments and sights at the guns were marked off in some decimal system which we never succeeded in understanding, instead of in degrees. There was therefore no way of getting the guns on to a target except by pointing or waving one's hat or some such pre-twentieth century method.

As for our torpedoes, of which we carried eight, they were, like the gunnery system, of a commercial type sold (by the great firm of Vickers) to all and sundry, but to my torpedo-men, used to Admiralty types, they were something of a closed book. We frankly did not care for them, particularly as their warheads—the business end—did not incorporate the safety devices which would prevent them exploding if struck by a bomb or shell. How right we were to view them askance was demonstrated later, in the Norwegian campaign, when a Polish destroyer armed with similar torpedoes blew herself in half as a result of a bomb hit on her torpedo tubes.

All these things were very trying, but in compensation, we had, to my delight, the latest asdic equipment, and we had a set of engines which sent us creaming through the water at 30 knots with hardly a tremor.

A few days after commissioning we found that the name of our ship had been altered to *Hesperus* which I found very much more attractive. A change of name is supposed to be unlucky but it certainly was not so for *Hesperus*, for whom indeed it was a second change as she had originally been christened with some unpronounceable Portuguese name. It was not, however, for reasons of euphony that her name was changed, but because *Hearty* was apt to be mistaken for *Hardy*—the destroyer leader which was soon to gain fame at the Battle of Narvik. Another of our flotilla named *Handy* was in similar trouble as in Morse code this was only one 'dot' different from *Hardy*. She was renamed *Harvester* and, like *Hesperus*, was to gain fame in the Battle of the Atlantic.

The first two ships of this flotilla of Brazilian H's to be completed were *Hesperus* and *Havant* and, pending the commissioning of the remainder, these two ships were ordered to Scapa Flow for anti-submarine patrols in defence of that great fleet anchorage. Our first duty of any interest, however, was of quite a different nature. *Hesperus* and *Havant* were ordered to proceed to Thorshavn, the capital of the Faroe Islands, where I was to inform the Governor that, to forestall a German move in the same direction, the Allies were intending to occupy his domain and that the cruiser *Suffolk*, with a token landing force of Royal Marines, would be arriving the following day. On arrival at Thorshavn, I took the Captain of *Havant*, Burnell-Nugent, with me and landed to seek the British Consul.

A very jovial crowd greeted us on the jetty and it was with difficulty that we managed to evade their hospitable intentions and make our way to the consulate. From there we were taken to the Governor's house and before I could attempt to get round to the matter in hand, Burnell-Nugent and I found ourselves in an atmosphere of hospitality and good will with drinks in our hands. The Consul managed to get across to the Danish Governor the purpose of our visit—news which momentarily dampened the atmosphere; but, calling for silence, the Governor made a little speech to say that he accepted the situation under 'force majeure', and the matter was not referred to again.

My official business completed, Burnell-Nugent and I returned to our ships and took them out on anti-submarine patrol pending the arrival of the *Suffolk*. The mission was in the tradition of more spacious days before wireless telegraphy and air travel and I enjoyed the old-world air of it all.

Meanwhile the Norwegian campaign had begun and *Hesperus* was detailed as part of the escort for the battleship *Resolution* which was going to Narvik to bring her 15-inch guns to the support of our troops ashore. In the fiords, we took up the job of patrolling the entrances against submarines, alternating with inshore patrols off the town of Narvik which was closely invested by Allied troops. Here we were able to give our guns' crews their first taste of action as we had *carte blanche* to open fire on any enemy troops or army vehicles seen on the move.

Perhaps the favourite occupation for all the ships at Narvik was trying to put a shell into the railway tunnel which housed mobile German field-guns. When they thought we were not looking, the Germans would run a gun out from the tunnel and fire a couple of rounds. Our object was to have our guns trained and ready to fire at this moment and we felt much like a cat at a mousehole. Our very sketchy gunnery control system mentioned above was a big handicap and, by the time we left the area we could not claim better than even honours.

My memory of those days is filled with the incessant ringing of alarm bells for air attack which, as there was practically no darkness at that season in those latitudes, could come at any hour of the day or night. At Narvik we were out of range of the German Stuka dive-bombers so the attacks were all of the high level variety.

The routine was to increase to about 20 knots and as the aircraft reached their dropping position—which we could fairly accurately estimate if we could not see the bombs leaving—to make a 90° alteration of course. If all went well, the bombs fell neatly where we would have been if we had continued on our course. Sometimes, however, there would be two formations attacking at once and I well remember on one occasion my First-Lieutenant, Lieutenant White, muttering 'Don't look round now, sir, but we are being followed.' A second or so later a stick of bombs fell abreast of us though far enough off to cause no damage.

Meanwhile the guns would blaze away vaguely in the direction of the enemy. Once when the gunlayers could not see the target I remember calling to them to 'aim at the sun', which was about as effective as anything else. Surprisingly, this ridiculous procedure on several occasions scared off an enemy attack, which was immensely good for our self-conceit.

After a number of such successes one inevitably achieved quite a reputation with one's ship's company for skilful dodging; this lost its relish when one found that every destroyer captain had a similar reputation in his own ship! One interesting discovery I made was that though everyone was scared while the bombs were falling, each one thought that he was unique in this. On going down to the wardroom on one occasion when we had been able to anchor for a brief spell, I remarked to my officers how it annoyed me to see them so calm amongst the bombs while I was shaking like an aspen leaf under cover of my duffel coat. There was a moment's silence and then a burst of laughter as someone said, 'But we have only just been saying how we envied you *your* calmness'. After this mutual revelation I believe we all found it much easier to take things light-heartedly.

I think the most unperturbed member of the ship's company was my sailor-servant, Able-Seaman Brown, who never failed to arrive on the bridge the instant the 'all clear' was sounded with a huge, steaming mug of tea and a beaming smile. He will always linger in my memories of those days and of other different days. Days of gale and roaring seas when Brown would miraculously arrive in my sea-cabin with hot meals, prompt to the minute in spite of the ship doing every thing but stand on its head. How he dodged the seas as he made his way forward from the wardroom galley I have never understood. I know that on one occasion at least he was hauled back inboard after being swept half through the berthing rails. But nothing would curb his enthusiasm. The skipper's meals, like the mails, must go through!

I hope he reads this tribute to him wherever he is, for I thought him the salt of the earth.

It was surprising how indifferent was the aim of these

high-level bombers even with stationary targets. The *Effingham*, flagship of Admiral Lord Cork and Orrery, was moored at Harstad not far from Narvik and used to be attacked almost daily, but I do not think she was ever hit. When I first arrived at Harstad and berthed *Hesperus* I was pleased to have found a comparatively open piece of water in which to anchor until some habitué of the place advised me that it was down wind of *Effingham* and bombs aimed for her usually arrived a few cables down wind as the German airmen seemed incapable of allowing for the effect of the wind on the trajectory of their bombs.

The time came for us to take part in an operation to land troops at the town of Mö, a fair distance south of Narvik. This took us within range of the Stukas and we found that they were a different kettle of fish. Our main armament of 4.7-inch guns could not elevate sufficiently to get them in their sights and we were left to depend upon one .5-inch multiple machine-gun of very doubtful reliability and a couple of stripped Lewis guns.

In all this time we never sighted a single allied aircraft though we were assured each evening by the BBC of what deeds of derring-do the RAF were performing all round us. While we were at Mö, however, the glad tidings filtered through to us that the aircraft carrier *Glorious* was in the vicinity and that we could count on air support. This was our downfall. When a flight of aircraft appeared in 'line astern' and with their undercarriages lowered—a recognition signal for our aircraft at that time—we took them for naval Skuas. It was not till they peeled off for their diving attack that we realised our mistake.[1] We managed to get sufficient way on to avoid any direct hits, but two near misses under our stern caused damage which restricted our speed and which required dry-docking for repair. So when a homeward-bound convoy was formed a week or two later we were ordered to form part of the escort and then to go on to Dundee for repairs.

[1] German Stukas had fixed undercarriages.

CHAPTER 2

Atlantic Battleground

MY ambition from the outbreak of hostilities had been to serve in the anti-submarine war wherever the enemy was thickest. When it became evident that the Atlantic was to be their chosen battleground I longed for the chance to join our then meagre forces fighting bitterly on the defensive.

I had a good reason for this. The hunt for, the stalking of, and the final killing of a U-boat had always seemed to me to be the perfect expression of a fighting sailor's art. Since the eclipse of the sailing ship the seaman's highly specialised talents had been steadily submerged in a welter of scientific and mechanical instruments to the extent that sea warfare had become largely a matter of mathematical computation, of aiming guns accurately at a barely-visible target some dozen miles away.

In anti-submarine warfare contact with the enemy would be at close quarters, and the fight would develop finally into personal combat in which good seamanship might well decide the issue.

As a junior commander, I had a horror of spending the war bogged down in a fleet destroyer as a solitary cog in a vast complex battle organisation, in which the chances of getting at the enemy were remote indeed. Perhaps I was deplorably lacking in the ability to submerge myself in the anonymity of fleet screening. Certainly I resented always being at the beck and call of those 'Big Brothers', the battleships and aircraft carriers.

In the winter of 1940, my unconscious desire for independence was fulfilled and, still in command of my destroyer, *Hesperus*, I was transferred to the Atlantic battlefield.

The first few months were disappointing. Contact with the enemy was rare mainly because of mistaken tactics employed by our command ashore. We were sent on one wild goose-chase after another to the positions of the latest sinkings only to find—as expected—that the guilty U-boat had fled the scene and was hidden in the deepfield.

It was one of the worst winters in living memory out in the Atlantic and we, like so many other escort and hunting ships, spent it mostly hove-to in appalling hurricanes, unable to make headway, while reports streamed in directing us to a U-boat attacking a lone merchantman or to a periscope allegedly sighted by a patrolling aircraft.

I well remember one of these barren patrols for the more than usually prolonged ferocity of the weather. *Hesperus*, in company with her sister-ship, *Hurricane*, was patrolling rather aimlessly, being directed from time to time on to the stale scent of a U-boat, when the barometer started on the downward dive that indicated an approaching depression. We were prepared therefore for a south-westerly gale but soon we realised we were in for something more than usually savage.

Wind and sea rose steadily and before long we were 'hove-to', just keeping the engines turning enough to maintain steerage way. This was normal in a severe Atlantic gale but conditions continued to worsen. The wind rose to a screaming madness; the terrifying rollers towered high above us with their tops streaming away down wind in spray.

Maintaining steerage way was a problem, for any forward motion meant that each monstrous wave struck us that much harder and the bow buried itself that much deeper into the wave's flank, scooping on to the deck tons of water which crashed their destructive way aft, wrecking any movable object in their path.

To move along the upper deck was to take one's life in one's hands and it was necessary to divide the ship into two sections, those aft not being allowed to come forward and those forward having to remain there.

The forward section of officers consisted of one watch-keeper and myself and for two days and nights we 'held the fort' alone up on the bridge, snatching food and sleep as and when we could.

With the gyro-compass out of action from the appalling shaking it received every time we slammed down into the trough of a wave, and the magnetic compass veering wildly from side to side, it was impossible for the helmsman to steer a compass course. Hour after hour the ship had to be conned by orders from the bridge to the man at the wheel down below, as we tried to keep her from falling away and getting beam-on to the seas.

But as the screaming squalls struck savagely at us, the rudder alone was insufficient steering aid and only by calling on the engines for short bursts of power could we keep heading up into the seas. This called for nice judgement, for if power were kept on for a fraction too long the thrusting propellers would send the ship crashing into an oncoming wall of water with appalling force. Attention could not be relaxed for a moment.

The dark hours were perhaps the most awe-inspiring, for all that one could see of the approaching seas was the white of their tops as they rolled over and broke. They seemed to be at an impossible angle above us and to be surely going to crash down to break us like an egg-shell.

On top of all this came blinding flashes of lightning, torrential downpours of rain and the eerie St Elmo's fires flickering at the masthead and yardarms and on any projecting object, at times even on the ends of our fingers and noses.

I remember at the height of this particular storm standing at the front of the bridge for hours on end, looking upwards at the tops of the waves rushing at us, and, as my gallant *Hesperus* faced each one, gripping the rail and crazily exhorting her to 'Climb, you—, climb!' Climb she miraculously did and we survived.

It used to put me in mind of the picture that hung in the cabin of my divisional commander when I had my first destroyer command, which showed a destroyer at sea in a gale and underneath the prayer: 'Ah! God be good to me. The sea is so big and my ship is so small.'

They were exasperating, futile days when the ships so badly needed to escort convoys were being battered by fruitless hunts in storm-swept seas, without any hope of reaching the enemy before he had slipped away into the vast blank spaces of the ocean.

But as that long and painful winter drew to an end it became clear to those of us at sea that the days of hopeless misemployment were coming to an end. For in February 1941, we felt for the first time the impact of Admiral Sir Percy Noble and his brilliant staff team, who had just set up their headquarters in Liverpool. They streamlined the organisation ashore and afloat, reorganised the ships and brought fresh thinking to the strategic battle plan.

A new feeling of intelligent purpose was in the air. Our sudden dashes across the ocean were not so aimless and each time we returned to harbour it was evident that head-quarters was more 'on its toes'.

There were plenty of rumours; but the one which proved of greatest interest foretold the formation of Escort Groups which would work-up and train together and remain as self-contained units. The object was to protect convoys with efficient teams rather than with groups thrown haphazardly together.

During February, Sir Percy Noble decided to go out into the Atlantic 'to see for myself how existing organisation can be improved'. By good fortune he chose to sail in a destroyer commanded by Commander Walter Couchman,[1] who was on this voyage senior officer of an escort.

Throughout the trip the escorts were subjected to all those interferences by the staff ashore about which we sea-captains had for so long felt bitter. The senior officer was unable to use his own judgement; the ships under his command were sent off on vain chases by orders from ashore, until eventually Couchman's ship with Sir Percy on board was left as the only escort to protect the convoy. No attack developed, but Sir Percy swore he would bring this nonsense to an end. It was a promise he kept and, by doing so, he laid the foundations of victory.

[1] Now Rear-Admiral.

On returning to Liverpool in March 1941 I was greeted with the news that I was to exchange commands. In place of my sleek *Hesperus* I was to take over an old, battered veteran of the First World War, the destroyer *Walker*. This was a rude shock. The crew of *Hesperus* and I had been through a lot together. The incessant air attacks of the Norwegian campaign and an Atlantic winter of unequalled ferocity had welded us into an efficient fighting team. I had no inclination at all to leave them and it was with a sad heart that I packed my bags and said good-bye to officers and men.

I could not have foreseen then that eighteen months later I was to return to *Hesperus* and with her enjoy the thrills of many striking actions against an enemy for whom the tide of victory was turning to defeat.

Meanwhile I took over the old *Walker* and a strange crew with some misgivings. She had been heavily damaged in a collision and had just been given a new bow. Such surgical operations are not always successful and I could not have the same confidence in her.

However, the pill was soon given a thick coating of sugar. With the command of *Walker* went command of one of the newly-formed escort groups. My job was to weld the ships into an efficient flotilla and take over the close escort of Atlantic convoys. This meant certain contact and action with the enemy and, when I discovered that *Walker* was a happy and experienced ship, my old confidence returned.

The officer with whom I was exchanging commands was an old friend and term-mate, Commander A. A. Tait, a gallant officer and brave man who subsequently became a famous Atlantic captain until his death in one of the most dramatic actions of the war.

The rush of turning over to each other made the stay in harbour all too short. Secret and confidential books had to be mustered and checked, stores accounted for and, when that was done, there was the business of attending convoy conferences with the masters of the merchant ships and reading sailing orders and convoy instructions.

But it was still early in March when I took *Walker* out of Gladstone Dock as leader of the 5th Escort Group, down the Mersey and out into the swept channel, where the convoy was already forming and heading for the Irish Sea.

The first few days with a convoy were always full of anxiety and activity for the escort commander. Anything from forty to eighty ships had to be counted, identified and checked by the convoy list; the inevitable stragglers who could not make the speed they had claimed at the conferences ashore had to be encouraged to do better or sent back to wait for a slower convoy; one or two ships would always break down with major or minor defects and a decision had to be made whether they should be left to rejoin within a reasonable time, whether an escort should be detached to protect them or whether they should be sent back to harbour for repairs.

Throughout this initial period, it was a rare treat for an escort commander to get more than an hour or so off the bridge at one time. Watch would follow watch and day would fade into night, but the escort commander, and usually his Yeoman of Signals, would continue at their post attending to the thousand and one little problems of a convoy getting into its stride.

The relationship between the convoy commodore and the escort commander perhaps needs explaining here. The commodores of ocean convoys were drawn from the ranks of retired admirals and senior merchant navy officers, who were given the acting rank of Commodore RNR. They embarked with a small signal staff in the ship selected as their flagship for the voyage and their duties were to ensure the internal discipline of the convoy and its safe navigation and to manœuvre the convoy as a whole, either to take it safely through restricted waters or, at the request of the senior officer of the escort, to evade enemy attack.

In theory, the escort commander was responsible only for the convoy's defence against enemy attack, but the dividing line between the spheres of responsibility was vague in the extreme. For example, a ship in the convoy improperly darkened was a matter of internal convoy discipline and if strict protocol were adhered to this would be dealt with by a request from the commodore to the escort commander to send an escort alongside her to remonstrate. But of course the culprit was exposing the convoy to danger from the enemy so any escort seeing such a breach of discipline dealt with it on the spot without reference to the commodore.

The commodores were vastly senior to the escort commanders and had they cared to stand on their dignity and insist on the letter of the law with regard to responsibilities, relations could have been very difficult. Fortunately they almost always behaved with wonderful courtesy and restraint and accepted the guidance and suggestions of their escort commanders who, they realised, were better informed of the general situation than they themselves were with their restricted radio communications.

There was indeed an obscure paragraph in the convoy instructions which did place the ultimate safety of the convoy as a whole on the shoulders of the escort commander and on the only occasion when I differed with my commodore it was a convenience to be able to invoke it.

On the occasion in question the convoy I was escorting was approaching home waters in dirty weather when I received a signal giving the position and course of an outward-bound convoy which, if we continued on our present course, would meet us head-on—a situation to be avoided at all costs. Giving the commodore my reasons I suggested he alter course to avoid it. I knew that I had an accurate position of our convoy on my chart as my navigator had managed to get a fix by the stars that morning, but the commodore preferred to trust the estimated position which was all his flagship's navigator could offer, and he declined to accept my suggestion. A series of more and more acrimonious signals then passed between us and it was a very angry commodore who finally accepted defeat.

But this was my only fracas with a commodore and on all the other occasions we parted company with expressions of mutual esteem. The country owes a lot to these gallant gentlemen, many of them well on in years, who came out of their retirement to lend the weight of their experience and authority in producing the wonderfully disciplined convoys which maintained impeccable formation in spite of every enemy effort to break them up. The roll of honour of the commodores who gave their lives in this service is long and distinguished.

Before it was clear of the Irish Sea and in the Western Approaches on the edge of the Atlantic, the convoy would steam in two columns often more than ten miles long until the ships could sort themselves out and maintain steady station-keeping at the right distance from the ships ahead.

Meanwhile, lamp and wireless communications had to be tested, guns exercised and convoy rituals performed, while the escorts barked around the convoy like sheepdogs. The clatter of signal lamps went on continuously from dawn to dusk when it would be replaced by the muffled clicking of the shaded night lamps. My tiny signal staff consisting of one Yeoman of Signals, Gerrard, and two Signalmen, Mortimore and Derbyshire, seemed never to sleep, for on them so much depended.

Poor visibility and an inky, choppy, black night would only add to the difficulties of sorting out those great collections of ships and increase the burden carried by the escort commander. There was no radar to help and all ships were strictly darkened—the use of navigation lights was forbidden for pressing and obvious reasons.

As the land dropped away astern and the open ocean was reached the convoy would be formed up by the commodore into eleven or twelve lines of ships covering an area about six miles across and two miles deep. The escort commander would then fling his half-dozen ships in a ring three to five miles outside the convoy. This ring formed a perimeter some forty-five miles long and escorts were therefore some eight miles apart.

Each ship would be allotted a section of this ring to patrol and, while the convoy steered a steady course, the escorts would weave back and forth across their area. Never on the same course for more than two minutes and never a regular pattern of zigzag was the golden rule to make things as difficult as possible for the U-boats.

In my sea-cabin under the bridge the endlessly repeated

orders to the quartermaster at the wheel and his replies formed, with the ping of the asdic, a continuous noise background, night and day, day after day, a background which I soon ceased consciously to hear and through which I could sleep soundly only to be instantly awake should the noise pattern vary. An undertone of urgency or anxiety in the voice of the officer of the watch, or an echo to the ping, would sound an alarm in my sleeping brain, and on many occasions I found myself halfway to the bridge before the reason for my waking had penetrated to my conscious thoughts.

At other times, lying awake, an unaccountable feeling that all was not well would seize me and, sure enough, on going aloft a sheepish officer of the watch would say, 'Sorry, Sir. We've got a bit out of station'; or perhaps, 'I'm afraid I've lost touch with the convoy. Visibility has closed in. I was just going to call you.'

Control of this widely spread force at once became a problem. In those early days the radio-telephone fitted in our ships worked on high-frequency or short wave which, unlike the Very High Frequency (VHF) sets which we had later, could be picked up at great ranges and so could be monitored by the enemy. It could not therefore be used for plain-language messages which could pass useful information to the enemy, except in emergency. Everything had to be laboriously coded and decoded or sent by visual methods.

Administrative and tactical signals had therefore, when possible, to be passed round the group and to the commodore of the convoy by signal searchlight during daylight. Hour after hour, the shutters of the lamps would clatter, passing messages to the next adjacent escort halfway to the horizon who in turn would pass it on to her neighbour. The tiny signal staff allowed in those days to the senior officers of escorts performed prodigies of efficient signalling in all weathers and every degree of visibility, as did the signalmen on the heaving, cavorting bridges of the little corvettes; and it was not often that, as darkness descended, there were still important messages outstanding.

But even so, how I longed for the VHF sets which were slowly coming into service! It was not until the American

VHF set known as TBS (Talk Between Ships) became available through Lease-Lend that our desires were met. The transformation the TBS worked in the cohesion of the group dispersed around the sprawling convoy was wonderful. Instead of the tedious process of call-up by lamp and the laborious spelling out of an order, or the shorter but insecure communication by HF radio, each ship was in immediate touch with the others by simply speaking into a telephone handset, the message coming through on a loudspeaker on the bridge.

Given this quick and fairly certain means of communication, not only were many weary hours of visual signalling eliminated, but prearranged tactics to deal with various emergencies could be carried out precisely and in concert, and the efficiency of the group as a team rose tremendously.

It was not without its drawbacks, however. Reliance upon it became so complete that the standard of visual signalling fell steadily and a breakdown of TBS sometimes left a ship virtually out of communication with her fellows. It had its dangers too. All ships were on the same frequency and one could unconsciously jam another. Nothing could be more frustrating than to have some important manœuvre hanging in mid-air while an interminable message from a neighbouring formation on some such triviality as fresh provisions would monopolise the air.

There were amusing aspects also. The differing accents of two signalmen on the TBS could produce moments of misunderstanding which would have brought the house down as a music-hall turn.

But all this was in the future and when I commanded my group from the *Walker* visual signalling was still the basis of control.

With such a loosely woven, extended force, it was of vital importance that it should have trained as a team and that each commanding officer should know what was required of him without the necessity for signalled instructions. Lack of these conditions time and again led to unnecessary defeats at the hands of the U-boats.

It was obviously useless to hope that such a scattered force would form a screen proof against U-boat attack. By zig-zagging independently around its allotted position, an escort could cover a considerable territory with the asdic, but on a dark night any well-handled U-boat could sneak un-detected between the escorts. On such nights zigzagging was impossible owing to the danger of collision. Only on moonlight nights could we get any relief from the strain of clinging to a convoy, and concentrate on detecting the enemy. For this reason I became almost a worshipper of the moon and to this day the sight of a new moon recalls those dark winter nights early in the war when a storm and no moon meant hanging on to the convoy in little more than two hundred yards visibility and hoping that all the ships would be with us when morning came.

Sometimes the merchantman I had decided to keep station on herself lost contact with the convoy and at dawn we would find just the pair of us alone in an empty, storm-swept ocean.

The strain of constant vigil was something the U-boats never had to worry about. When submerged their hydro-phones told them of a ship's presence at a considerable range; then they could surface and carry out an attack with all eyes thoroughly rested.

Fortunately no attack developed during my first outward bound voyage as escort commander and I was given time to study the many problems which would arise when the enemy made contact. Often I spent hours on the bridge, or in the chartrooms, discussing tactical operations with my officers in the hope that someone would come up with an answer. But by the time we had dispersed our convoy about six hundred miles out and set off to rendezvous with another in mid-Atlantic for the return trip, we had still not worked out a satisfactory counter-attack. When the time came, circumstances would have to dictate my action.

I was comforted somewhat to learn that most of my officers in *Walker* were experienced professional seamen, accustomed to searching dark horizons, while I myself was blessed with splendid eyesight and had many years of night exercises behind me. There was every hope that should a U-boat attack in our sector of the screen we could spot him before he penetrated into attacking range.

My First-Lieutenant and asdic officer was Lieutenant J. C. Langton, a former P & O Line officer who was a fine seaman and navigator.[1] Lieutenants Peter Sturdee RN and Rupert Bray, Sub-Lieutenant Ronnie Westlake RNVR, R. J. Chaplin, Gunner (T) and Midshipman R. B. Mann RNR completed the team of executive officers in which I quickly realised I could have the utmost confidence in an emergency.[1]

My engineer officer was Mr G. F. Osborne, Commissioned Engineer, who had nursed the ageing machinery of *Walker* since the beginning of the war and kept it running in fair weather and foul with amazing reliability—a feat which we only really appreciated when we heard how other ships of the same vintage got along. The life of an engineer in those old ships was one long succession of patching up worn-out steam joints and coaxing tired machines to behave as their makers meant them to. It took real engineers to avoid breakdowns under these conditions. 'Chiefy' Osborne, his Chief Engine-Room Artificer Paine and his Chief Stoker Lugger certainly qualified for the title, for never once did *Walker* let me down.

Rendezvous with a convoy in mid-ocean was an event full of drama which, to me, never lost its thrill though I experienced it dozens of times. In the usual dirty Atlantic weather the navigational problem was always difficult. Either the convoy or ourselves, or both, might have been for long days of storm with no sight of the sun or stars from which to obtain an accurate position.

The usual scheme to ensure a meeting in bad weather was to head first for the 'furthest-on' position that we estimated that the convoy could have reached. There the flotilla would be spread at something more than the visibility distance and would sweep down the track of the approaching convoy. This allowed for considerable errors of navigation. An anxious period ensued, with all eyes straining through the

---

[1] Langton was killed later in the war; Bray and Sturdee are now Commanders; Westlake later commanded a submarine.

murk to catch the first glimpse of the grey shape of a merchant vessel looming up. Sometimes the convoy would have been delayed much more than estimated and hour after hour would go by while I would anxiously wonder whether the convoy had passed by unsighted and was maybe now steaming further and further away as each minute passed. Suddenly the radio telephone would crackle and the blessed news would come in that one of the flotilla was in sight of the convoy. A wave of relief would flood through my mind as all ships of the flotilla swung inwards and moved to their pre-arranged screening positions round the convoy.

In fair weather the difficulties were not so acute, but the meeting was in some ways even more dramatic, as on this occasion, when early on 15th March, 1941, my searching eyes saw the forest of top-masts rise over the western horizon, and I knew our rendezvous had been well made. The ships were then some fifteen miles away, but gradually, as the range closed, the whole stately array of them came into full view—some fifty merchantmen carrying supplies and munitions to a lonely beleaguered Britain.

My escort group consisted of, in addition to my own ship, the destroyers *Vanoc*, *Volunteer*, *Sardonyx* and *Scimitar* and the corvettes *Bluebell* and *Hydrangea*.

I took *Walker* over to the commodore's ship, exchanged signals and the usual gossip of the sea. Number 25 had broken down four hours ago and was steaming to catch up; but would she make it before nightfall, or should she be sent off on a straggler's route well clear of the convoy, to avoid the risk of her leading a U-boat to the convoy's whereabouts?

Number 53 had developed stearing gear trouble and had been put to the rear of a column to give her more sea-room for manœuvring. A member of 37's crew was seriously ill and would have to be transferred at sea to an escort carrying a doctor. In another ship a man was suffering from some lesser complaint and we would steer alongside her so that our doctor could advise the ship's captain over the loud-hailer on the proper treatment. At such times the conversation would prove highly diverting.

These chores took up most of the day with my group

patrolling their stations to ward off unexpected daylight attacks. All the while the convoy was heading for home—and into a dangerous concentration of U-boats.

The code name for our convoy was HX 112 and, as we steamed eastwards, I wondered if those gallant merchantmen knew how ill-equipped their escort really was to deal with a determined attack. For them, any moment might bring a torpedo crashing home; then a crowded lifeboat in a freezing winter ocean could be the best they could hope for. I swore to myself that if I couldn't prevent the enemy from attacking, I would do everything humanly possible to avenge the victims.

By nightfall we had received enough warnings to indicate we had been spotted by the enemy and were now being shadowed. I warned my ships to prepare for an attack after dark, and a cloak of tense expectancy settled over the convoy.

We had not long to wait.

CHAPTER 3

The Fate of Three Aces

DURING the summer of 1940 and on through the winter, our convoys had been suffering crippling losses in the North Atlantic. The escorts, weak in numbers and lacking training as teams, seemed unable either to prevent these losses or to avenge them.

In Germany, three outstanding U-boat commanders were credited with the majority of these losses. The Germans are more given to hero-worship than the British, and these three 'aces' were the toast of all Germany and the recipients of the highest decorations. On return to harbour they would be greeted by their commander-in-chief in person, bands would play triumphal marches and their crews would be wafted away to the earthly Valhallas of rest camps or to winter-sports resorts at public expense.

These three heroes were Günther Prien, commanding *U 47*, Joachim Schepke of *U 100* and Otto Kretschmer of *U 99*. Prien had first made his name by his brilliant exploit in penetrating the defences of Scapa Flow and sinking at her moorings the battleship *Royal Oak*. A consummate seaman, a ruthless fighter and an ardent Nazi with more than his share of personal conceit, he was a brilliant individualist as a U-boat commander. By March 1941 he was credited with having sunk about 245,000 tons of Allied shipping.

Schepke, with 230,000 tons, was of different character. Debonair, happy-go-lucky, with something of an actor in his make-up, he was more than ready to play the part of the hero, with his cap at a rakish angle and an attitude of supreme self-confidence.

The third and most successful of the trio, Otto Kretschmer, was the most dangerous enemy of them all. Utterly fearless, supremely confident of his skill as a seaman and a fighter and devoted single-heartedly to his career in the navy, he commanded his U-boat with the iron hand of a martinet, bringing his crew to the highest pitch of efficiency, yet earning their complete devotion. Not for Kretschmer the boastful speeches, the theatrical gestures, the contemptuous over-confidence in the face of the enemy. His equals found him hard to know, nicknaming him 'Silent Otto'. The hero-worship which was showered on him and the glamour which his name evoked were equally distasteful to him. Compared with his exuberant fellow aces he seemed a sinister figure. Out in the wastes of the North Atlantic he and *U 99* were indeed a sinister and deadly menace, and no less than 282,000 tons of shipping had been sunk by them.

Each of the three 'aces' had thus sunk more than 200,000 tons and they had an agreement that the first to reach 300,000 should be wined and dined by the other two. In the early days of March 1941 they slipped from their moorings at Lorient and headed back for the convoy routes. For the first time all three were at sea together. As *U 99* sailed, the strains of the 'Kretschmer March', composed by the Army bandmaster in his honour, could be heard across the waters of the harbour.

But even the great are mortal and the legend of indestructibility which surrounded these three men was about to be shattered.

Filthy weather plagued escorts and convoys from the North Channel across the wide sweep up to Iceland. Huge, menacing seas rose high above the ships to crash down on creaking, groaning decks; men with red, bleary eyes strained to peer through the curtain of drizzle; and low overhead the dark water-filled clouds threatened fresh misery every dawn.

There was no escape from it. They had to stick it out and concentrate harder than ever lest some lurking enemy should slink through their screen and decimate a helpless, wallowing convoy,

But the U-boats were not so harassed. When the strain took too heavy a toll on tired nerves, they dived to the peaceful protection of the world below the surface, safe in the knowledge that our asdics were unreliable in the weather 'upstairs' and, in any event, the operators would have lost their keen sensitivity in the wretchedness of their sodden, heaving surroundings as watch followed watch with never a let-up in the weather.

Prien crossed the path of an inward-bound convoy about two hundred miles south of Iceland and took his chance, He drove in shortly before dusk on the 10th, the great seas hiding *U 47's* tiny silhouette. But for some freakish reason a rain squall scurrying across the scene suddenly cleared, leaving behind it a patch of passably good weather with decent visibility. To her horror *U 47* found herself in full view of a destroyer.

For a shocked second the hunter and hunted gazed at each other in surprise. Then *U 47* heeled over in a tight turn as Prien attempted to run away on the surface. The destroyer— HMS *Wolverine*, commanded by my old friend, Commander Jim Rowland—increased to maximum speed allowed by the weather and gave chase.

Then Prien made his mistake. He dived and, in doing so, lost speed and manoeuvrability. *Wolverine* raced over the diving spot and dropped a pattern of depth charges at shallow setting. Down below, the U-boat heeled and shuddered under the shock, and an ominous rumble developed from her propeller shafts. The explosions had blown her propellers out of alignment, thereby creating the danger that at any moment the engines would be torn from their mountings. To a submarine hoping to remain submerged this would be disastrous; for she needs to make headway through the water to maintain her depth.

Prien decided to take another chance. He would surface and rely on the darkness, just fallen, to hide his escape. It would be just too bad if the engines failed him. He surfaced about a mile from *Wolverine's* starboard bow, out of sight in the murky visibility. But his damaged propellers were clearly audible on *Wolverine's* asdics.

Jim Rowland resumed the chase and again Prien was forced to dive. This time the depth charges caught him on all sides, blowing in the sides of his ship. A tremendous underwater explosion accompanied by a vivid red flash told the tale of success to *Wolverine* and, a few minutes later, wreckage coming to the surface brought confirmation.

The first of the aces had been destroyed. Kretschmer and Schepke would be liable for only two bottles of champagne—if either should return to Lorient.

By the 12th the weather had eased, although rain squalls were frequent and there was no escaping the bitter east wind. Kretschmer in *U 99* and Schepke in *U 100* had encountered and sunk several convoy stragglers and had been part of a pack which had attacked an inward-bound convoy.

They had lost contact with each other but destiny had decreed they should meet at HX 112, as we made our way eastwards towards the danger zone created by the depredations of the aces.

Schepke reached us first. Shortly before midnight on the 15th he approached on the surface from the starboard side of the convoy. He crept to within a mile of the beam screen and fired a 'fan' of four torpedoes at the long line of overlapping silhouettes. Two minutes later the *Erodona*, a 10,000-ton tanker carrying petrol, burst into blinding flame casting a ghastly glare over the heaving waters. Then came the dull detonation of the torpedo striking home. I had never before seen this most appalling of all night disasters and on the bridge of *Walker* we were shocked into silence by the horror of it and the immediate thought that none could possibly survive.

Alarm bells clanged urgently through the ship and sent men running to action stations. In the glare from the blazing tanker we searched desperately through our binoculars for the sight of the U-boat responsible, while we zigzagged widely to cover as much sea as possible. Nothing was to be seen and the asdic ping brought no answering echo to indicate that we had detected a submarine under the surface. Silence from the other escorts showed that they were being no more successful. The corvette *Bluebell* was ordered to close the sinking tanker and see if there were any survivors to be picked up, but she soon reported that the sea was ablaze with floating petrol and that not a soul could be alive.

There was no way of telling whence had come the torpedo. The U-boat might have fired from any point of the compass or it might be right in amongst the convoy columns. The escorts were stationed so as to cover as far as possible any direction of attack.

To our astonishment and relief, however, the night wore on with no further attack and the coming of dawn brought us temporary relief.

Yet I could not help but look forward to the next night with a deep sense of anxiety. My untried team were quite certainly going to have a battle on their hands—would my first report as a group commander consist of a sad tale of sunk or crippled ships with no U-boat 'kills' to offset the losses?

We waited all through the daylight hours, tensed and ready and it seemed as though the shadow of impending doom hung above the convoy. Then shortly before dusk a signal flashed from *Scimitar* on the port bow of the convoy: *To Walker—From Scimitar. Submarine in sight six miles ahead.* Even as I began giving orders a wave of relief poured through me. At last we could get to grips with the enemy. I ordered full speed ahead and as signals streamed from my bridge, I was joined by *Vanoc* and *Scimitar*.

As we closed the distance, the U-boat dived while still three miles away, and I spread out my small force in a line abreast one and a half miles apart so as to cover him with our asdics in whichever direction he might have gone. There seemed every reason to hope that, with the scent so fresh, we might make a 'kill' and we started our hunt with keen anticipation. But we searched vainly until the approach of darkness made it imperative that we rejoin the convoy—and not so much as a trace of a decent echo. Leaving *Vanoc* and *Scimitar* to continue the hunt for a further two hours, I took *Walker* back.

However, we had kept the enemy submerged, and now a drastic alteration of course by the whole convoy put him well astern. It would take him most of the night to catch up and regain an attacking position. I could hardly hope that he would be the only attacker, and I was sure the night held action in store for us. But I did not yet know that we were up against the cream of the U-boat arm—a weak, loosely-knit few against Germany's most famed aces.

Leaving *Vanoc* and *Scimitar* to keep down our elusive enemy, I raced back to the convoy and regained station at 10 p.m. Six minutes later, my expectations were fulfilled by a brilliant flash and loud explosion on the other side of the convoy.

Our evasion tactics had failed: battle had been joined for the fate of HX 112.

In the next hour, five ships were torpedoed. I was near to despair and I racked my brains to find some way to stop the holocaust. While the convoy stayed in impeccable formation, we escorts raced about in the exasperating business of searching in vain for the almost invisible enemy. Our one hope was to sight a U-boat's tell-tale white wake, give chase to force her to dive, and so give the asdics a chance to bring our depth-charges into action. Everything had to be subordinated to that end and so, with binoculars firmly wedged on a steady bearing, I put *Walker* into a gently curving course, thereby putting every point of the compass under a penetrating probe. It worked.

As her bows swung, a thin line of white water came into the lens of my glasses, a thin line which could only be the wake of a ship. There were none of ours in that direction; it had to be a U-boat! I shouted orders increasing speed to 30 knots and altered course towards the target. Suddenly, the U-boat spotted us and in a cloud of spray he crash-dived. A swirl of phosphorescent water still lingered as we passed over the spot and sent a pattern of ten depth-charges crashing down. We could hardly have missed; it had been so quick we must have dropped them smack on top of him. Then the depth charges exploded with great cracking explosions and giant water spouts rose to masthead height astern of us. Two and a half minutes later another explosion followed and an orange flash spread momentarily across the surface. We had every reason to hope that this was our first 'kill'.

Though we learned later that this was not so, for our charges had exploded too deeply to do him fatal damage, we felt almost certain at the time when our asdic search showed no trace of a contact. *Vanoc* came racing past to rejoin the convoy and offered assistance. I refused this, convinced as I was that we could safely leave the scene with a 'probable' marked down in the log book, and ordered her back to her station.

However, no U-boat was officially recorded as destroyed without tangible evidence and I continued the asdic search until such time as wreckage should come to the surface.

It was just as well. For half an hour later we gained contact with a certain U-boat. Our prey had not been 'killed'; he was, in fact, sneaking back towards the convoy still bent on attack.

Recalling *Vanoc* to assist in the hunt, we set about our target with a series of carefully aimed patterns of depth-charges.

Taking it in turns to run in to the attack, pattern after pattern of depth-charges went down as we tried to get one to within the lethal range of about twenty feet of our target. But he was a wily opponent and, dodging and twisting in the depths, he managed to escape destruction though heavily damaged.

Soon the waters became so disturbed by the repeated explosions, each one of which sent back an echo to the asdic's sound beam, that we could no longer distinguish our target from the other echoes and a lull in the fight was forced upon us.

I had for some time past noticed in the distance the bobbing lights from the lifeboats of one of our sunken ships, but with an enemy to engage there was nothing for it but to harden my heart and hope that the time might come later when I could rescue the crews. This lull seemed a good opportunity and perhaps if we left the area temporarily the U-boat commander might think he had shaken us off and be tempted into some indiscretion. So, the *Vanoc* steaming round us in protection, we stopped and picked up the master and thirty-seven of the crew of the SS *J. B. White*.

This completed, the time was ripe to head quietly back to where the U-boat had last been located and perhaps catch him, licking his wounds on the surface.

We had hardly got under way when I noticed that *Vanoc* was drawing ahead fast and thought perhaps she had mis-read the signal ordering the speed to be maintained. As I ordered a signal to be made to her, Yeoman of Signals Gerrard said, 'She's signalling to us, sir, but I can't read it as her light is flickering so badly'. I realised that *Vanoc* must be going ahead at her full speed and being, like *Walker*, an old veteran, her bridge would be shaking and rattling as her 30,000 h.p. drove her forward through the Atlantic swell.

Rupert Bray, on the bridge beside me, said, 'She must have sighted the U-boat.' Even as he spoke, *Vanoc* came on the air with his radio telephone, with the laconic signal: 'Have rammed and sunk U-boat.'

What a blissful moment that was for us, the successful culmination of a long and arduous fight. Something in the way of revenge for our losses in the convoy had been achieved.

There was grim joy on board *Walker*, and not least amongst the merchant seamen from the *J. B. White* who felt they had a personal score to settle. But for the moment our part was confined to circling *Vanoc* in protection, while she picked up the few survivors from the U-boat and examined herself for damage. We were glad of this breathing space as, with all the depth-charges carried on the upper deck expended, the depth-charge party led by Leading-Seaman Prout were struggling to hoist up more of these awkward heavy loads from the magazine, with the ship rolling in the Atlantic swell, and often with water swirling round their waists. They were not a moment too soon, for, as we circled *Vanoc*, I was electrified to hear the asdic operator A. B. Backhouse excitedly reporting 'Contact, Contact'. But I could hardly credit it, for not only was it unbelievable that in all the wide wastes of the Atlantic a second U-boat should turn up just where another had gone to the bottom, but I knew that there were sure to be areas of disturbed water persisting in the vicinity from our own and *Vanoc's* wakes. The echo was not very clear and I expressed my doubts to John Langton, but Backhouse was not to be disheartened. 'Contact definitely submarine,' he reported, and as I listened to the ping the echo sharpened and there could be no further doubt. With a warning to the men aft to get any charges ready that they had managed to hoist into the throwers and rails, we ran into the attack. It was a great test for John Langton for, with the maddening habit of the beautiful instruments of precision provided for us, they all elected to break down at the crucial moment. But much patient drill against just such an emergency now brought its reward. Timing his attack by the most primitive methods, Langton gave the order to fire. A pattern of six depth-charges—all that could be got ready in time—went down. As they exploded, *Walker* ran on to get sea-room to turn for further attacks, but as we turned, came the thrilling signal from *Vanoc*—'U-boat surfaced astern of me.'

A searchlight beam stabbed into the night from *Vanoc*, illuminating the submarine *U 99* which lay stopped. The guns' crews in both ships sprang into action and the blinding flashes from the 4-inch guns and tracers from the smaller weapons made a great display, though I fear their accuracy was not remarkable. Destroyer night gunnery in such a mêlée is apt to be pretty wild and, in those days when flashless cordite was not issued to us, each salvo left one temporarily blinded. In *Walker* confusion soon reigned around the guns for the enthusiasm of our guests from *J. B. White* knew no bounds. Joining up with the ammunition supply parties, shells came up at such a phenomenal rate that the decks were piled high with them till the guns' crews were hardly able to work their guns. But fortunately we were able very soon to cease fire as a signal lamp flashing from the U-boat, 'We are sunking' (*sic*), made it clear that the action was over. Keeping end on to the U-boat in case he still had some fight left, we prepared to lower a boat in case there was a chance of a capture, but even as we did so the crew of the U-boat abandoned ship and she plunged to the bottom.

I manœuvred *Walker* to windward of the swimming Germans and, as we drifted down on to them, they were hauled on board. Some of them were in the last stages of exhaustion from the cold of those icy northern waters by the time we got them on board. Some indeed would never have made safety had not Leading-Seaman Prout gone over the side fully clothed to aid them. One was so apparently dead that he was nearly consigned to the deep there and then but someone suggested trying to thaw him out in the warmth of the galley—and in due course he came to life. This man, a Petty Officer named Kassel, later proved invaluable as an interpreter and go-between and lived to have some strange adventures as a POW.

The last to come over the side was obviously the captain, as he swam to *Walker* still wearing his brass-bound cap. We were soon to find out that we had made indeed a notable capture, for the captain was Otto Kretschmer, leading ace of the U-boat arm, holder of the Knight's Cross with Oak Leaves and top scorer in terms of tonnage sunk. As he reached our deck an amusing little incident took place. Kretschmer found to his surprise that he still had slung round his neck his Zeiss binoculars, a very special pair made at Doenitz's orders for presentation to a selected few aces. Kretschmer had always sworn that no enemy would ever board his ship and no enemy would get these prized binoculars. The first he had ensured and now he tried to send his glasses to the bottom also. But he was too late. Peter Sturdee grabbed them and in due course they arrived on the bridge, where I claimed them as my prize of war. For the rest of the war they were my inseparable companions and played their part in bringing several of Kretschmer's successors to a similar fate.

Meanwhile the convoy, free at last of its persecutors, had steamed on and it was time for us to rejoin. Even as we set course, we thought for a moment that more attacks were developing, for a look-out suddenly shouted, 'Flares, bearing Green 10'. However, a quick look showed that it was the waning moon climbing out of the sea to the eastward and the tension worked up in all of us collapsed in a gale of laughter. The St Patrick's Day which had started so grimly had seen revenge come to sweeten our bitterness.

From my post on the bridge, news came to me from time to time of how our prisoners were behaving as they recovered from their shock and exposure. Kretschmer himself was confined to my after-cabin where he sank very soon into the profound sleep of exhaustion. Of the remainder, only the First-Lieutenant, von Knebel-Döberitz, behaved in the arrogant way we had learnt to expect from dyed-in-the-wool Nazis and had to be put firmly in his place from time to time.

Papers found on some of the prisoners were cuttings from German magazines lauding the exploits of the U-boat men whom they called 'sea wolves'. Another document of great interest was a drawing showing a convoy with, in its midst, a U-boat firing torpedoes into the ships at point-blank range. This indicated that Kretschmer's tactics had been to do just that. Confirmation came from the Master of the *J. B. White* who had indeed sighted *U 99* between the convoy columns and had been turning his ship to try to ram when he had been struck by two torpedoes and brought to a standstill. We began to realise then why all our desperate vigilance had been of no avail once the attack had started, for it became clear that all the damage had been done by the one boat, *U 99*, and she was out of our reach in the middle of the convoy. The other U-boat sunk had evidently been the one sighted on the previous evening. Having evaded our search, it had steamed at high speed on the surface to overhaul the convoy and so betrayed itself by its conspicuous white wake. What happened to the three other U-boats which prisoners stated had been co-operating, we never found out, but they certainly failed to bring off an attack. Perhaps our sharp alteration of course after dark had shaken them off as so often in other encounters.

At daylight it was possible to exchange signals freely with Jim Deneys in *Vanoc* and our satisfaction was intense when we heard that the other victim had been *U 100*, commanded by Joachim Schepke, second only to Otto Kretschmer in fame as a harrier of our shipping. Two aces in one night was a considerable bag. *U 100* had been forced to surface by *Walker's* and *Vanoc's* attacks and was hoping to escape on the surface, having been, as he thought, given up by us. The need for relentless and persistent hunting of a U-boat, which was always being dinned into us, was thus amply demonstrated. One significant feature of the action was that *U 100* had been detected, for the first time in history, by the primitive and till then largely ineffectual radar set in *Vanoc*.

The last moments of *U 100* had been grimly dramatic. When Schepke in the conning-tower saw *Vanoc* tearing towards him, he called down to his men: 'All right, he will miss us astern.' No doubt he was deceived by *Vanoc's* camouflage painting, for a few seconds later he died horribly, crushed between the destroyer's bow and his own periscope standards.

During the day we overhauled the convoy and as we steamed up the lines, our prisoners were brought on deck to have a look. It was comical to see the look of dismay on their faces as they saw the splendid array of ocean-going ships, steaming in perfect formation as though nothing had happened. Our hearts warmed to those gallant masters who had grimly stuck to their station in the convoy, when every instinct must have been urging them to slide off in the darkness away from the danger area—a seemingly sensible act which in practice meant almost certain disaster.

Kretschmer, also on the quarterdeck at this time, was seen to be staring with lively interest at the ship's crest, a horseshoe. Turning to 'Chiefy' Osborne standing by him he remarked, 'This is a strange coincidence! My ship also sailed under the sign of the horseshoe, though ours was shown with the points downwards.'

'Well, Captain,' replied the Chief, 'in our belief a horseshoe that way up allows the luck to run out and it would seem in this case to be only too true,' which brought a rueful laugh from our prisoner.

Meanwhile on board captives and their capturers settled down together more or less amicably in the very restricted space available; for it must be remembered that besides almost the whole of *U 99's* crew we had on board the crew of the *J. B. White*. These felt that they had a personal score to pay and at times had to be restrained from taking it out of the Germans. There was no question in my small ship of keeping the prisoners segregated. The wardroom was very congested with the officers from the *J. B. White*, the Germans and my own officers who could barely find space for themselves when off watch. While the Germans were thawing out, John Langton, anxious not to have pneumonia cases on his hands, ordered whisky for the Germans. Von Knebel-Döberitz haughtily refused his drink, pompously ordered the remainder not to drink with us, and ended with a Nazi salute and a 'Heil Hitler'. Mr Chaplin, the gunner, was on to him like a terrier and warned him that if he valued his life that was the last time he would try on anything of that sort. The others were told to drink up and after a slight hesitation they did so and tension relaxed. The merchant navy officers could not resist some minor digs at the Germans. While their uniforms were being dried off, not only the medals and insignia were taken as souvenirs but even the fly-buttons. Great were the complaints when the Germans discovered their losses. The rules for treatment of POWs forbade the confiscation of medals and insignia and Peter Sturdee had quite a job extracting them from their purloiners to return them. The flies were never recovered and I never did hear how the Germans managed without.

With the congestion in the wardroom, the senior members of our guests were given my harbour cabin to use. My engineer officer, Mr Osborne, a devotee of contract bridge, soon got a four going, consisting of himself, Kretschmer and the master and chief officer of the *J. B. White*, an extraordinary combination when one thinks of it, with the addition of an armed sentry to add piquancy. Osborne always maintained that it was the only time in the war he managed to get a decent game!

From Kretschmer we were able to discover very little and we were for a long time puzzled as to why he had blundered into us in the way he did. Had he a rendezvous with *U 100* astern of the convoy, or was he trying to come to the aid of his comrade? Long afterwards I learnt the truth from Kretschmer's own account and realised how lucky I had been. For *U 99*, with all torpedoes expended, was looking forward to nothing but a quiet passage home and the usual rapturous welcome. Kretschmer had no inkling that he was anywhere near any escort and was himself below, when, steaming fully surfaced his officer of the watch suddenly sighted *Walker* or *Vanoc* and crash-dived immediately. As usual, the U-boat had had the advantage of the first sighting and, had he stayed on the surface, might well have made off unseen. As it was, submerging at once made him detectable on our asdics and his fate was sealed. This also explained how our first detection was very uncertain, no doubt just as the U-boat was diving; but as it went deeper it was fairly caught in the asdic beam and clearly identified. Kretschmer himself laments the decision of his officer of the watch to dive, which was strictly against his standing orders for action in case of a sighting. But the sands of his luck had truly run out that night from the upside-down horseshoe that was the badge of *U 99*.

Kretschmer gave us the impression of being far from the fanatical Hitlerite we had half-expected. Indeed, as a professional naval officer and a most skilful one, he had much the same attitude to politics as we had ourselves and preferred to restrict himself to his duties and lament the mess the politicians had made of things. Kretschmer spoke good English and knew the West Country well, having studied at Exeter University for some time before the war. He professed to admire our people and was bitter that the activities of politicians had made it necessary 'for the only two decent nations of Europe to fight each other'. One cannot help wondering whether the revelations of the horrors perpetrated by his countrymen at Belsen and such-like places have modified this rather naïve summing-up of the situation![1]

The next day the convoy had reached the sheltered waters of the Minches and could safely be left to the remainder of

---

[1] Admiralty records of Kretschmer's interrogation by Intelligence Officers say: 'The capture of Kretschmer and loss of *U 99* . . . is a serious blow to German morale and propaganda and an important victory for Britain over the U-boats. The crew of *U 99* gave the impression of having attained a higher degree of efficiency than any other U-boat crew interrogated so far. For the first time there was no criticism of officers. On the contrary a marked degree of loyalty and admiration for their captain was expressed by the men. He was less of a Nazi than had been assumed.'

the Group to escort. *Walker* and *Vanoc* were ordered ahead to land their prisoners at Liverpool. From the urgent signals calling for details it was clear that our success had made something of a sensation at home. At last the long run of failures to counter the U-boats' night attacks had been broken. Though it was not solely responsible for the success, the fact that, for the first time, a U-boat had been detected by radar was an indication of things to come and pointed the way to the cancelling-out of our disadvantage at night *vis-a-vis* our elusive opponents.

Our arrival in Liverpool was something of a triumph. My battered and salt-stained little ship was berthed at Prince's Landing Stage, usually reserved for more lordly vessels and we were greeted by the C.-in-C. Sir Percy Noble and many of his staff, all anxious to give us their congratulations.

CHAPTER 4

Life with the Convoys

JUBILANT as I was with the result of my first convoy battle and more than ever confident that my escort group and my ship were becoming a team, well-trained and competent, I knew, too, how much there had been of luck in our success. Schepke had died, true to form, through over-confidence. Long immunity had led him to underrate the possibility of being sighted on the surface at night and, steaming at high speed, his wake had given him away and from that moment he could be brought within asdic range. Against a skilful team his doom was then certain. We could not hope for others to make the same mistake.

Kretschmer, by sheer bad luck, had stumbled into the asdic beam of a destroyer when, as he thought, the battle was over, the convoy passed on and nothing but a quiet passage to Lorient lay before him.

The U-boat properly handled in night attack had still an immense advantage, though *Vanoc's* radar detection of *U 100* gave promise of a turn of the tide. Furthermore we knew that Kretschmer had been using the tactics of penetrating between the columns of the convoy, into a position from which he could pick his victims with certainty and with no possibility of a miss, whilst enjoying virtual immunity himself. Submerged or trimmed right down, he could maintain the speed of the convoy, and remain unsighted.

Had the German U-boat arm maintained the high standard of its early days, it would seem certain that it would have continued to use bold tactics of this nature. Rapid expansion, however, and this loss of the three aces within a week, led the Germans to turn instead to mass attacks, popularly known as the 'Wolf Pack' tactics. These tactics entailed a rigid control of all U-boats by HQ to ensure a concentration round each convoy before an attack was launched. In the event, the Germans to some extent played into our hands by this decision, for it meant that any U-boat commander making a first sighting of a convoy had to report the fact to the shore and then remain shadowing until a wolf pack had gathered. If the time to attack had come, he had again to break wireless silence and report the fact.

One of the scientific developments of the Second World War was the perfection of a direction-finding apparatus capable of accurately taking the bearing from a ship of a high frequency wireless transmission. In my *Hesperus* we had had one of the first of these sets, but initially results were very poor and unreliable. The later sets which were installed in our escorts were a great improvement and it will be seen later how this device and the German propensity for radio 'chatter' led directly to the destruction of a number of U-boats which would otherwise have remained undetected. I have no hesitation in saying that High Frequency Direction Finding or H/F D/F played as great a part in the defeat of the U-boats as did radar, though of course one was complementary to the other and each served to bring into play the ultimate killer, the asdic.

But these developments were still in their infancy and until they reached maturity it was the human eye alone which could seek out at night the submersible torpedo-boat which is what the German night tactics had made of the U-boat.

The arrival of spring and summer allowed us to peel off some layers of the warm but damp clothing in which we lived continuously at sea during the winter. The behaviour of some ships in convoy was as unpredictable and uncertain as ever and gave us plenty of headaches, but of the enemy there was hardly a sign. The award of a batch of decorations to various officers and ratings of *Walker* and *Vanoc* was a cause for gratification, though, as always on these occasions, it was sad that only a few members of what was essentially a team could be singled out for them.

On return from one trip, during which we had had as our guest in *Walker* the distinguished American author and lecturer, Vincent Sheean, we arrived in Liverpool to find it in the throes of its 'blitz'. On our first night there took place what we knew as the Battle of Bootle, when that part of the Mersey port was badly hit and some thirteen merchant ships in the river and docks were sunk. But for some reason, when the German Air Force had Liverpool at almost its last gasp, the attack was shifted elsewhere and the port was able to get into its stride again.

Peter Sturdee had a lively night in charge of the ship's fire party dealing with the incendiaries which came down in showers. Vincent Sheean, determined not to miss anything, joined up with the party and provided considerable light relief at times. Lacking experience at that time of air raids his reactions were slow and as Peter and his party dived for cover to the tune of the whistling bombs, Sheean would be left standing, a large and solitary target, only to dive madly in his turn just when the danger was momentarily over. But he bore a charmed life and emerged unscathed, perhaps made immune, we thought, by the intensity of the celebration of our return to harbour earlier in the evening, which had left him in that happy condition in which one has the special protection of the 'Cherub up aloft', so sailors say!

Gladstone Dock, the basin in which all Liverpool escorts berthed, received a number of hits, including one which wrote off my car—to my intense disgust—but the ships were very little damaged. However, two of the three lock gates of Gladstone Dock were damaged and another hit would have either imprisoned the escort fleet in the basin or would have made the basin tidal so that we should have then all rested firmly on the bottom at low water. We were therefore all sent off to base ourselves on Londonderry.

We were quite familiar with the outer approaches to this Northern Ireland port for, in the estuary of the River Foyle, was stationed a tanker from which escorts could take a last drink of oil fuel before setting out into the desert of the Atlantic Ocean. We were therefore used to lying close off the neutral shore of Eire whence 'bumboats' would ply a trade with us in such rarities as fresh eggs and nylon stockings. The fact that sometimes only the top layer of eggs was fresh, or that the life of the stockings was very short, did not greatly upset us for an egg was an egg in those days and nylons a sure way to a girl's heart.

Now, however, we had the experience, familiar to other escort groups already based there, of threading our way up the narrow and tortuous channel of the River Foyle to the historic old city of Derry. On our first arrival there, I embarked a pilot and invited him to con us up the river. To my dismay, being properly brought up in the methods of navigation and pilotage as taught at HM Navigation School, I found that the compass was ignored by this intrepid old gentleman, who preferred to steer on such objects ashore as 'Mother Murphy's white cow' or 'Paddy Monaghan's byre'. With a shudder of horror I instructed John Langton to extend the hospitality of the wardroom to the pilot while I reverted to more orthodox methods of pilotage.[1]

Londonderry was a land 'flowing with milk and honey' for us, where such unheard of luxuries as steaks could be had in the restaurants and butter in lumps instead of thin slivers. After the scenes of smoking ruin at Liverpool, Londonderry's peaceful air, where people would probably show you the scene of the explosion of 'the bomb' was a benison. It sometimes made going to sea to face the winter gales all the harder. As one slipped down the narrow river, peaceful little sheltered cottages passed within biscuit toss. The blue peat smoke rose lazily into the air and one envied the owners their warm fireside and quiet night ahead of them. A corner of the river would be rounded, the wind would start keening through the rigging and we knew that by nightfall water would be sloshing about between decks and we would be lashing ourselves into our bunks when the time came to turn in.

The summer months of 1941 constituted almost a lull in the Battle of the Atlantic. Although our convoys still suffered attack and our losses in merchant ships continued, the U-boats had lost some of their confidence and if they found a convoy well escorted they would withdraw to find easier

---

[1] I would like to say that after the war I was again based at Londonderry and found that the present generation of pilots are right up-to-date and smart as paint.

prey or their attack would be half-hearted. On two occasions the convoy escorted by my group suffered casualties but never on the scale inflicted by such aces as Kretschmer and Schepke. In each case the attack was beaten off for the loss of one ship of the convoy but the U-boat responsible escaped.

On one of these occasions *Walker* had an interesting duel with a U-boat in which, though it is sad to relate the U-boat escaped, valuable clues to the tactics and capabilities of submerged U-boats were discovered. On 26th July, 1941, the outward-bound convoy OS 1, escorted by my group, was attacked in daylight by a submerged U-boat and the SS *Atlantic City* was torpedoed and damaged. Knowing that the submarine with its slow submerged speed must eventually drop astern of the convoy after its attack, I organised a search in that direction and soon was lucky enough to pick up a contact on the asdic which we confidently assessed as being a submarine.

We prepared to use depth charges and *Walker* ran in for the first attack. To our dismay, the contact was lost when we were still some five hundred yards away, which meant that the attack had to be delivered largely by guesswork and on the assumption that the enemy continued at the same course and speed as had been calculated during the early part of the run-in. We began to doubt also whether our contact was indeed a submarine, or could it be one of those maddening shoals of fish which so often gave an echo to our ping, only to disperse and vanish when attacked? Still, we had to make sure and our depth-charges were duly delivered at the estimated time and place to cover the U-boat.

Running on and turning back to pick up the contact again in the position indicated by our automatic plotting table, we drew blank and our doubts increased. But when a wider search was made, there was the firm solid contact again with all the characteristics of a submarine under way. Confidence restored, *Walker* ran in again to deliver a careful, accurate attack; but once again contact was lost at five hundred yards or so and when next picked up the target was far from where it was calculated it could be in the time.

It was clear we were up against a U-boat with capabilities

of deep-diving and rapid manœuvre greater than any with which they had been credited to date. The range at which contact was lost was an indication of great depth of target, for the asdic beam was fixed 'in elevation' and, like that of a searchlight, able to sweep round but unable to be raised or lowered. Thus, as the target was approached, it came steadily into an increasingly narrower part of the beam until, at a range dictated by its depth it passed out of the beam altogether and no echo came back to the asdic receiver.

To lose contact at 500 yards meant that the U-boat was at some 600/700 feet depth and our Intelligence at that time gave the limiting depth to which they could go as 350 feet. On this assumption, our depth-charges were so designed that the deepest at which they could be set to explode was 500 feet.

Similarly, Intelligence had led us to believe that the standard U-boat's turning capabilities were equivalent to those of our own submarines. But when the contact was regained after each attack, the target turned up in a position which indicated it had been able to manœuvre with a much greater agility. There we were, with a nice fat U-boat on the end of our asdic beam and unable, with the weapons at our command, to deal it a fatal blow. Throughout a long, warm, summer morning, in a calm sea, we and our consort, the Norwegian destroyer *Bath*, tried to outguess the U-boat commander's manœuvres and, if we could not get our depth charges down to his depth, we hoped we might at least make them explode accurately above him.

To our rage and shame the U-boat sailed serenely on its way in the depths until our depth-charges were all expended. Even so, could we have held contact we might have called for others to continue the attack and finally have forced the submarine to the surface when his batteries were exhausted. Unfortunately, the asdic had one serious limitation. If the layers of water near the surface of the ocean became heated or chilled to any great extent, the sound beam became distorted, and could finally become diverted at a steep angle to the bottom of the sea or to the surface. The hot summer sun blazing on a strangely calm Atlantic was steadily producing these conditions as the morning wore on and, towards noon, we realised we had lost contact. Frantic search, wider and wider in scope, produced no result and we knew we had been finally defeated.

An escort with no depth-charges was of little value with a convoy and, in any case, our convoy was by now nearly out of the danger zone, so with permission from the command we hurried back to Londonderry to replenish. Here we were able to put in our report. U-boats were diving to 600 feet or more and could turn submerged in tighter circles than a destroyer. This information was greeted with considerable scepticism but when, in August of that year, *U 570* fell intact into our hands, it was found to be true. As a result depth-charges capable of being set to sink to 700 feet before exploding were eventually devised and issued to the escort forces.

The problem of delivering these depth charges to the correct spot still remained unsolved, however, until the late Captain Walker, our foremost U-boat killer, devised what he called the Creeping Attack which I was able to use later in the war to good effect.

As the summer wore on, with only sporadic attacks being made on our convoys, it would seem that an excess of confidence beset the staff at Derby House. The essence of convoy protection, the escort flotilla, kept together as a trained body and under a commander whose tactical ideas were so well known to his captains that in action few orders were needed, was gradually abandoned under the stress of finding ships to undertake the countless tasks for which destroyers and corvettes were wanted.

The group I commanded became more and more diluted and dispersed. This was not always the fault of the directing staff. The hazards of wartime navigation in congested waters and under 'black-out' conditions were very real and sometimes instructions, which were intended to give one the advantage in the presence of the enemy, were blindly followed when the dangers of encounter with the enemy were greatly less than the normal sea hazards. One destroyer of my group disappeared from the scene for many months under repair, through head-on collision with another destroyer in the narrow straits joining the Irish Sea to the North Channel. Both ships were steaming at 20 knots, completely darkened and without navigation lights on a pitch dark night.

In such a situation the danger of navigation lights aiding an enemy was remote, and it would have been a wise precaution to have shown them. Other ships suffered heavy-weather damage through wrong-handling in the enormous Atlantic seas and in retrospect it is clear that guidance for the inexperienced, based on the lessons learnt in the first winter of the war, would have helped to avoid many such incidents and lessened the chronic shortage of escorts from which the Western Approaches was never free.

Whatever may have been the chief cause, as the autumn of 1941 approached with its longer nights and the prospect of a renewed onslaught on our convoys, the system of properly constituted escort flotillas had largely broken down. My own group finally broke up when *Walker*, becoming due for a refit, went to Southampton in September for the purpose and the ship's company went off, a half at a time, for some well-earned leave.

I had been for some time engaged to Monica Strickland and on 11th November we were married at Brompton Oratory. We had met in the hectic first months of the war when the destroyer I commanded, *Venomous*, was engaged in the nightly cross-channel escort of the troops to France. Since then our courtship had been carried on at such far-apart places as Dundee, Southampton, Kendal and Liverpool. The absence of any long leave and the inability to forecast the brief leaves between trips had always prevented any plan being made for a wedding.

With my ship in dry-dock at Southampton we were able to honeymoon in the New Forest and I could keep an eye on my ship at the same time. I fancy that my wife then learnt to accept the hard lesson that a naval officer is never heart-whole if he has a ship to care for, and she soon came to accept and indeed to understand this.

With the end of the honeymoon *Walker* was again ready for sea. The most important addition to her armament was a structure like a miniature lighthouse above the bridge—our new type radar.

Radar was the perfect complement to the asdic which would revolutionise the situation round the convoys. Where the asdic failed so lamentably, in detection of submarines on the surface, radar was to fill the gap.

Given this magic eye, it would become impossible for a surfaced U-boat to penetrate the screen of escorts undetected, no matter how black or wild the night. Moreover, if knowledge of our possession of radar could be kept from the enemy for a while, he would be walking blindly into a trap if he maintained his tactics of surface attack. For surprisingly although the Germans had been ahead of us in the development of radar for gunnery control in large ships, they had not envisaged its use in aircraft and escort vessels and for a long time they were completely puzzled as to what means of detection was causing so many of them to be surprised on the surface by night.

Our earliest radar sets had been highly unreliable and barely capable of detecting a submarine sooner than could the eye. *Vanoc's* detection of *U 100* at one mile was an outstanding performance and not to be expected. But with the new sets now coming into production, ranges of three or four miles could be obtained.

A further refinement of radar sets as they developed was the Plan Position Indicator (PPI), which gave a continuous visual presentation of the area round the ship on which any object detected by the radar showed up as a blob of light. This completely solved the old, harassing problem of night escort, for a picture of the whole convoy and its escorts was always on display on the PPI and a glance at it would betray immediately any alteration in the convoy formation or any shifting from her station of an escort. Previously, with the onset of darkness the escort commander had no knowledge of what might be going on in the convoy. No longer now was the attention of the officer of the watch distracted by having to keep the convoy in sight, even on the blackest night. The PPI did this for him and he could concentrate on detection of the enemy.

The relief to escort group commanders and to all their escorts' captains was inexpressible. No longer the anxious nights of storm and blackness when it was as much as could be expected of the escort to keep perilously in sight of the nearest ship of the convoy, looming vague and menacing a few hundred, spray-swept yards away. No longer that helpless, intimidating realisation that the first warning of a night attack would probably be the thud of a torpedo striking home in the convoy and the distress rockets from the victim soaring up into the sky.

It was not at once that these improvements reached us, of course. The products of the back-room boys came to us bit by bit, but the new set installed in *Walker* was an enormous advance.

With this exciting new device we were more than ever keen to get back into the Battle of the Atlantic and we set off for Liverpool confident that convoy duty awaited us.

My wife had gone ahead to get rooms in the Mersey area so that we could be together during my brief stays in harbour. What was my dismay, therefore, and that of my ship's company, when as we shaped up to enter the Gladstone Dock an excited figure on the dock wall bellowed at us to go to sea again and that orders were being signalled. The orders when they arrived could not have been more unpopular. They were for us to proceed to Iceland where we were to relieve a destroyer of the Home Fleet as part of the screening force for the capital ships based on Hvalfiord. For me this was the most depressing prospect.

Instead of my cherished independent command and the prospect of renewing our duel with the U-boats, I foresaw weeks of lying at anchor waiting for the unlikely chance of the big ships getting into action with a German unit breaking out into the Atlantic. How right my forecast turned out!

Christmas came and New Year and still we lay in that dismal Hvalfiord where night began at 3 o'clock and daylight at 10, the only excitement being the daily emergency and shifting of billets as the sudden winter gales came screaming down the fiord. We thought our purgatory was at an end when our two battleships raised steam and put to sea, with us duly taking up our position on the screen, and set off south-eastwards towards home. But alas, we soon learned that two other battleships were taking their place and on meeting we were to transfer ourselves to the new squadron and return to Iceland. We felt we were truly the forgotten men and, being Western Approaches ships working for the Home Fleet, we felt we might never get back to our own hunting-grounds.

CHAPTER 5

Transatlantic Respite

OUR Iceland exile came to an end eventually, of course, and we found ourselves back at Liverpool for a brief spell in February 1942. But instead of the expected return to the Atlantic convoys *Walker* received orders to cross the Atlantic to Canada to be based on Halifax, Nova Scotia.

This brought one of our pleasanter interludes for we had to put in to Punta Delgarda in the Azores for fuel. As it was a neutral Portuguese port, our stay was strictly limited, but it was blissful to be able to relax in the atmosphere of peace. The British Consul kindly invited some of my officers and myself to luncheon in his flower-decked house and regaled us with some of the local wines.

But before we could altogether relax there were the age-old courtesies of the sea to exchange with the Portuguese guard ship at anchor in the harbour. This meant a ritual call by my officer of the guard and a search for a sword for him to wear. This weapon, so readily available in time of peace, paradoxically was conspicuous by its absence in wartime.

However, one was finally unearthed and Rupert Bray, correctly accoutred, pennant flying from the bows of his boat, made the call and was received with the time-honoured ceremony of twittering pipes and saluting officers, though the solemnity of the occasion was somewhat marred by the passing of bottles of port wine down to my boat's crew by the Portuguese sailors, anxious to demonstrate their status as Britain's oldest allies.

On arrival in Halifax, we found that we were to lead a group of what was to be known as the Western Local Escort Force. Disappointed as we had been to be removed from our old stamping-ground, news of the U-boat operations on

56

the American east coast soon made us realise that we had in fact come to the area in which we were most needed.

For the United States, at war since December 1941, was giving the U-boats a field of operations which became known to them as the U-boat paradise. Woefully short of all types of escort vessel, and with no convoy organisation previously planned, the Americans hoped that strategically placed striking forces of fast submarine chasers and aircraft would be able to inflict heavy losses on the U-boats should they attack the shipping routes on the US east coast, even though ships were allowed to sail independently.

As the majority of these shipping routes run close inshore for a great deal of their length, such a belief would have been understandable had there not been shining examples of its fallacy both in the First World War and on the British side of the Atlantic in the Second. Human nature being what it is, it would not have been surprising had the Americans merely been unprepared to base their strategy on the experience of others, particularly if those others were at all ready to suggest that having been already at war for two years they 'knew all the answers'. But in fact these mistaken beliefs were contrary to the advice given by their own experts—the Support Force which had been entrusted with the anti-submarine campaign in the Atlantic. Using the technique of escorted convoy, this Force achieved the remarkable result in the same period of escorting some 2,600 ships with the loss of only six.

Their own great Fleet Commander of the First World War, Rear-Admiral W. S. Sims, USN, was also an authority the Americans might have accepted, and by doing so, have saved themselves and their allies from shipping losses of appalling magnitude. Admiral Sims wrote of the U-boats:

'Our tactics should therefore be such as to force the submarine to incur this danger in order to get within range of merchantmen. It therefore seems to go without question that the only course for us to pursue is to revert to the ancient practice of convoy. This will be purely an offensive action because if we concentrate our shipping into convoy and protect it with our naval forces we will thereby force the enemy, in order to carry out his mission, to encounter naval forces. . . . At present our naval forces are wearing down their personnel and material in an attempted combination of escorting single ships, when they can be picked up, and also of attempting to seek out and offensively engage an enemy whose object is to avoid such encounters. With the convoy system the conditions will be reversed. . . . In a word, the handicap we now labour under will be shifted to the enemy; we will have adopted the essential principle of concentration while the enemy will lose it.'

But despite such a clear and authoritative warning, shipping along the American coast, which included a high proportion of valuable oil tankers carrying the very life-blood of modern war, continued to sail independently. By March 1942 the figures of merchant ship losses had sky-rocketed to the record monthly total of 500,000 tons. In that month the first convoys were organised. They sailed between Boston and Halifax without a single loss. But south of Boston, no convoys were run and by June losses had reached an all-time high with 700,000 tons lost in a month. Meanwhile, it was not until April that the first U-boat was sunk in the area. No wonder the U-boat crews afterwards referred to this period as 'the happy times'! In June the first convoys to and from the oil ports of Trinidad and Aruba were run—and not one ship in those convoys was lost.

By now the lesson had been well and truly rammed home —but at what a cost! As each portion of the shipping routes was included in the convoy system, the U-boats moved further afield in search of softer nuts to crack. And to point the moral for all time, the United States Naval Commander-in-Chief, Admiral Ernest King wrote:

'I might say in this connection that escort is not just *one* way of handling the submarine menace, it is the *only* way that gives any promise of success. The so-called patrol and hunting operations have time and again proved futile.'

Though at first American susceptibilities would not countenance the use of our ships off their coasts, with the organisation of a complete convoy system the anti-submarine forces of all the Allies were made interchangeable. This was after I left *Walker*, however, and while I was with her our area of operations was between Halifax and Newfoundland. In those icy northern waters all shipping was already organised in convoys, and there was 'no enemy but winter and rough weather'.

I suppose that by this time I was beginning to suffer from the strain of continuous sea command in war for more than two years, including two winters in the North Atlantic in small ships. Existence at sea was confined to the open bridge or the little box underneath it graced by the title 'Captain's Sea Cabin'. One was rarely dry in winter and usually miserably cold, in spite of layers of sleazy 'warm clothing'. The conditions off Newfoundland in winter were possibly more continuously foul than anywhere else I had served and the bitter cold which caused a layer of ice even on the inside of the ship's side, helped to wear one down.

The Plimsoll mark on the side of a merchant ship shows the draught to which it may be loaded under varying conditions. The line showing the least draught and so the greatest factor of safety is marked with the ominous letters WNA—for Winter North Atlantic. It is not surprising, therefore, that in the Winter North Atlantic the little corvettes and destroyers of the escort force took a considerable beating from time to time. Or perhaps it is truer to say that in destroyers the ships and their crews took a beating, while in the corvettes, owing to their wonderful sea-keeping qualities, it was only the crews who suffered.

The Flower Class corvettes of 1,010 tons, mass-produced for the sole duty of convoy escort and which, after 1940, formed the greater portion of any escort, were remarkably successful. In weather in which destroyers with their long sleek lines, designed primarily for speed, would be restricted to courses which would keep them heading into the seas to avoid serious damage or risk of capsizing, the Flowers with their broad beam would ride the huge waves with confidence and steer in any direction with safety. This did not mean, of course, that they rolled any less. They had a vicious roll which it took a strong stomach to put up with. But on the whole, destroyers, with their corkscrew motion, the crash of their bows as they smacked down with each wave that passed under them and the whipping of the hull as their screws rose to the surface, were more wearing to the bodies and souls of their inhabitants. And they were wet! With the 'hogging' and 'sagging' of their long hulls of thin, riveted high-tensile steel, small leaks would develop everywhere. Their fine, high-speed lines would cut through waves over which other types of ship would ride and the green water would then roll its destructive way along the forecastle and crash down on the iron deck. Or sometimes a sea would seem, without reason or warning, to rise up out of the general turmoil to windward and hurl itself vindictively down on the deck amidships.

Under these conditions, taking over or going off watch was an adventure. One careless move, a mistake in judging when the next sea would come aboard or perhaps a foolhardy dash for shelter scorning the use of the lifelines could result in a man being swept overboard never to be seen again. If conditions got too bad, all movement on the upper deck would be forbidden and in anything like bad weather no man would be allowed out of shelter alone. Disasters, of course were rare, but what was almost invariable was a thorough soaking which meant misery for those going on watch. For those going below it was little better for there is little opportunity to dry clothes on the mess-decks and a sailor cannot take many changes of clothing to sea with him, for lack of stowage space. In spite of continual baling and mopping, water would be sloshing across the mess-decks from one side to the other as the ship rolled. Conditions in wardroom and cabins were little better and it is perhaps worse to have a bunk from which you can be hurled to the deck from time to time than a hammock.

In the North Atlantic during winter such conditions sometimes continue for weeks on end. Depression follows depression with monotonous regularity giving no respite to dry out clothes or the ship between one screaming gale and the next. It would not have been surprising if morale had dropped, petty irritations grown into flaming rows, dislikes into hatred

—in fact, if all the symptoms of an unhappy ship had developed. But I heard of few such cases. Somehow the miseries shared welded ship's companies as a rule into happy teams.

It had not crossed my mind that I was near the cracking point. But one black, stormy night, we were approaching the harbour of St John's, Newfoundland, when my signal staff made some small error in exchanging recognition signals with the Port Signal Station. My Yeoman of Signals, Gerrard, was a man of unfailing good-humour and quiet efficiency, but I was furious at the mistake and gave him a scathing 'blast'. I realised later that this was entirely unreasonable and unjustified and resolved to try to control myself better in future, but at the same time I began to wonder whether I was heading for that psychological condition known as 'operational fatigue'.

It seemed too providential to be true, therefore, when I arrived in harbour to find my old friend and term-mate, Jim Rowland, Prien's killer, waiting to relieve me of my command. On relief I was to go to the new US naval base at Argentia as the British representative.

I left for Argentia with only the vaguest idea of what my job was to be. Indeed, I had never heard of the place before and it was not till later that I learnt that its harbour had been the scene of the historic meeting between President Roosevelt and Mr Churchill at which the principles of the Atlantic Charter were first enunciated.

Now it was to take its place in the history of the war as the forward base for the American contribution to the Atlantic battle, the 'Support Force' as it was known. From his headquarters at Argentia the US Admiral commanding this force controlled the convoys and their escorts while they were in the western half of the Atlantic. Responsibility passed from this American commander to the C.-in-C. Western Approaches at a position in mid-Atlantic known as the CHOP line.

Here at Argentia, too, the British and Allied escort groups

were to be based for their turn-round between convoys. For St John's, the capital of Newfoundland, used by the Canadian Groups, was too small to take any more.

So out of nothing a base was to be created. The dock facilities, the repair shops, the supply organisation and the refuelling arrangements of old-established ports like Liverpool or Greenock, as well as a full-sized air station, had to be provided in a few months. It was a project to daunt the heart of anyone accustomed to the orderly and deliberate progress of peace-time civil engineering. But to the Americans, with their tireless, New World enthusiasm and utter disregard of the cost, it was just another job.

Before their arrival Argentia was a tiny village, huddling round its tiny Roman Catholic church, and did not even give its name to the bay on which it stood, which was called after the neighbouring larger village of Placentia. By the time I arrived all had been transformed.

The Americans had set-to to carve a base out of the wilderness with all their customary hustle and vigour which was later to become so familiar but which, to my unaccustomed eyes, was a source of wonderment. Monstrous 'diggers' clattered furiously away all day and on through the night under the glare of arc-lights. Roads were laid down with the speed of an unrolling carpet and as often as not vanished again equally quickly when their purpose had been achieved. I well remember being bidden to dinner in the Admiral's mess one night and finding, when I wished to return to my own quarters, that the road by which I had come had vanished like a dream. As the 'Flag Mess' was 'dry' in accordance with US naval custom, I needed a very strong restorative to recover from the shock when I got home.

There were other amusing aspects of this furious activity. For instance, there was a local legend that the first digger to be set to work to excavate the peat moss to prepare a foundation for the first runway of the airfield, could find no solid bottom and finally dug itself underground and was seen no more. And time and again the power supply of the base would fail as some juggernaut would plough its way madly through the underground electric cables—a little co-ordination between departments having been overlooked. On one occasion the water tank just above my quarters collapsed with a most spectacular smash which any small boy would have given his soul to see, and a torrent of water swept round the house which, being made of wood, I expected at any moment to become water-borne.

Later on, a project to excavate for the installation of underground oil-tanks was set in motion round the 'British Embassy', as my quarters were called by the Americans, and day by day we found these vast pits encircling us more and more and creeping nearer and nearer, till eventually one narrow path alone kept us in communication with the outside world. I used to wonder whether the engineers in charge were using a map which did not show my house, and I feared that some day my staff and I would be swept unnoticed into the belly of some mechanical Moloch and that only our absence from the club that evening at 'gin time' would reveal the disaster that had overtaken us.

When I first reported at Argentia I found that Lieut.-Commander Alison was holding down the job pending my arrival, but he could not enlighten me as to what my position was in this 100 per cent US base. The job itself was plain enough. It was to look after the interests of the British escort groups which were now accompanying the convoys the whole way across the Atlantic and using Argentia as their base for replenishment and repair before returning with a homeward-bound convoy. But how I was to achieve my object was not so apparent, for I was not appointed to the staff of the US Admiral or the CO of the base who would supply our needs. As the solitary 'Limey' in the place—my staff were at first all Canadian—I was looked on with the utmost suspicion. Had I come to try to teach the Americans their jobs? Or would I claim the right to participate in the operational control of the British ships which, in the western half of the Atlantic, came under US naval control? At this stage of the American participation in the war, that close liaison between our navies, almost integration indeed at times, which became common later, had not yet been achieved.

The US Navy very naturally feared that with two and a half years of war behind us we might be prone to claim that our experience gave us the right to lay down the law in operational matters. My welcome by the senior US naval officer, Admiral Bristol, was therefore hardly cordial and his chief of staff, Captain R. B. Carney, later to rise in a meteoric career to be Chief of Naval Operations of the US Navy, managed to convey—in the nicest possible manner—that I had better stick to my purely administrative desk and leave operational matters alone.

There were amusing sides to the situation. I remember my desperate struggle to be allowed to see signals concerning the movements and expected arrivals of escort groups, so that I could arrange for their reception, berthing and replenishment. These signals were 'operational' and so outside my province. But I finally convinced the American staff that the nature of my job really did necessitate my having this information and that the simplest way of passing it to me was to let me see the signals. Even then, 'security' imposed a ban on my being given copies and I had to go, cap in hand, to the Flag-Lieutenant to beg for what I needed. Eventually this problem sorted itself out and I well recall the day when a vast and complicated safe was installed in my office so that these secret documents could safely be left in my hands.

I confess that I was somewhat chilled by this reception, but the wonderful experience of being once again in a land where there was no black-out and where meat was a thing which came by the pound and not by the ounce, and of being able to go nightly to a bed in which I did not need to wedge myself in to prevent being thrown out, was sufficient compensation and gave me patience to await the time when this early chill might wear off.

In the event, the time was to come when I was able to count 'Mick' Carney as a great personal friend and to have a real affection for the rest of the Admiral's staff.

As to the job of seeing to the welfare of the escort groups, it was made easy by the open-handed generosity, the passion to be of service, and the slick efficiency of the US Navy. The repair and maintenance of our ships were centred in the repair ship USS *Prairie* which was also the flagship of Admiral Bristol. The equipment of this ship, and above all the enthusiasm and brilliant organisation of her ship's company, were an eye-opener to me and to the escorts which were looked after by her. I had had some experience of our own repair ships and they came very badly out of the comparison.

Perhaps because the US Navy, unlike the Royal Navy, has never been able to count on dockyards and bases constantly under their lee in foreign waters, they have developed to a fine art the employment of the mobile 'fleet train' of repair and replenishment ships. The Royal Navy could do worse than take a leaf out of their book in this matter and thus restore to the fleet some of the mobility lost since the mechanical age put ships at the mercy of repair facilities outside their own resources.

I shall always look back on my time at Argentia as a wonderfully peaceful interlude in an otherwise incident-packed war. Between visits of escort groups, when the harbour was empty of British ships, I was not exactly heavily occupied. Mick Carney had arranged for a little wooden house, very typical of Newfoundland, to be set aside for my staff and me, and there we set up our own mess. Food was obtainable on the lavish American scale and our liquor and cigarettes were duty-free. At times my conscience stirred very slightly at doing so well when things were so grim at home, but I did not allow it to spoil my enjoyment which I felt sure was only an interlude.

I remember the horrified comments from my wife in reply to a letter in which I described fishing for trout through the ice of the frozen lakes, using raw steak for bait. I suppose the hook held more than her daily ration at home.

Not long after my arrival we were all deeply shocked by the sudden death of Admiral Bristol. He held a very high reputation in the US Navy and his loss was greatly mourned. In his place we got as our new Task Force Commander, Admiral Brainard, a man of great charm and kindliness with whom I instantly felt at ease.

The staff did not greatly change and, besides Mick Carney, the officers with whom I had chiefly to deal were Commanders Wooldridge and Ingersol[1]—both of them rather confusingly nicknamed 'Slim'—and Logan McKee. All subsequently obtained Flag rank. Logan McKee, an engineer officer, was told off specially to work with me, and I soon had a great admiration and affection for him. He was a first-class professional engineer and a man of infinite patience and good-humour. Nothing was too much trouble for him in seeing that our ships' lightest request was looked after.

Soon after my arrival, a considerable upheaval in administrative arrangements resulted from a momentarily alarming disaster. The wooden jetty at which lay the repair-ship *Prairie*, upon which the whole of the maintenance facilities for our ships depended, caught fire from a leak in the supply pipe through which petrol was being pumped. The wharf was very soon an inferno and the fire quickly spread to the *Prairie* which was secured more with an eye to the fury of the winter gales than to the possibility of a quick getaway. Heavy ship's anchor cables ran from her bow and stern to the shore and in the heat and confusion it was a long business getting her free, by which time the fire had got a fairly firm hold. For my part, I was chiefly interested in what was going to happen in two British corvettes, moored to the jetty under the bows of the *Prairie*. Their large deck armament of depth-charges would be engulfed by the fire if steam could not be raised for their main engines in record time.

There was nothing I could do but to keep my fingers crossed and to wonder whether depth-charges would burn or explode. I am glad to say I never found out, as the race was won by a short head—the paint on the depth-charges was already blistering.

The *Prairie* was considerably damaged by the fire and I wondered how the Americans would cope with our maintenance and repair problems in the future as the shore workshops and stores were still uncompleted. I need not have worried. With a whisk of the magician's wand, the Admiral's

[1] At present (1956), Commanding the U.S. Seventh Fleet in the Far East.

staff pulled another equally well-equipped repair ship out of the bag.

But the fire had one good result as far as I was concerned. It forced the Admiral and his staff to move to a shore head-quarters where they not only could set up a much more convenient communications organisation, but where they became a great deal more accessible to me.

I remember Mick Carney being at first horrified at the thought of a 'Stone-frigate' for the flagship, but I think he came to appreciate the convenience of it eventually, and of course it became a commonplace later in the war for flag officers to exercise their command from ashore.

By this time the bitter Newfoundland winter was beginning to slacken its grip on the land. Lakes and rivers unfroze and the iron-hard frost-bound 'muskeg' or peat moss, of which the countryside chiefly consisted, became an impassable morass. The road connecting Argentia with St John's, the capital, was little better than a cart track through the wilderness and liable to every form of blockage until the Americans, with typical energy and thoroughness, put their road-making teams to work and had a metal-surfaced road in use in an incredibly short time. This had one great incidental advantage: it made more accessible the splendid fishing available in the lakes and rivers. Being a passionate fisherman myself, my every spare moment was fully occupied.

I soon found that Mick Carney shared my passion, though he was quite out of my class as a fisherman, casting the most expert line it has been my pleasure to see. The fishing fever caught on and many were the happy days I spent with the Admiral and his staff out in the unspoilt wilds of the country-side. In this way I soon became accepted as one of them-selves—or so I flatter myself.

Indeed, Mick Carney seemed to think I was an essential part of his expeditions as he claimed he never caught any fish until I had managed to fall in, which I am ashamed to say I seemed to do with great regularity. However, the 'hot bourbon and butter', to which I was introduced an an anti-dote to ice water down my neck, mad excellent amends for my discomfort, so everyone was happy.

But though I had been taken to the bosom, so to speak, of the US Admiral and his staff, I am afraid that some of the officers of the naval base never agreed that I was a necessary evil. A feud, almost on Scottish lines, developed between the executive officer of the base and me and my staff. Many were the traps and obstacles laid in our path and we were kept constantly 'on our toes'; but with the Admiral and Mick Carney to back us and Logan McKee acting as a much-harassed cushion, we were fairly immune from the slings and arrows of our enemies.

I was nearly snared, however, on one memorable occasion when the base laid on an air-raid practice. I failed to realise with what thoroughness it would be carried through—we were some three or four thousand miles from the nearest enemy territory—and I was caught driving my station wagon with its lights on by a heavily-armed patrol. Only by hurriedly taking refuge in 'the British Embassy' did I escape a 'night in the brig'.

The crime was duly reported to the Admiral and a highly amused Mick Carney rang me up to inquire what I thought he should do about it. I assured him I had taken the severest disciplinary action with myself—and I heard no more about it.

As spring gave way to the blazing Newfoundland summer, it was clear that the mid-Atlantic where the British escort groups operated was becoming a battle centre again. The Americans were mastering the protection of their coastal shipping routes and the U-boats were not finding those waters the soft spot they had been. I began to get restive to be back in the thick of things and started to send home requests for a sea-going command again.

I was promised a relief 'in due course', but when at the end of June Commander Willy Orpen, commanding my old ship *Hesperus*, was promoted to Captain I begged to be allowed to relieve him. To my joy I was told that when *Hesperus*' Group (Escort Group B2) next called at Argentia I was to take passage home in her and relieve Orpen on arrival. In my place was to come Commander J. E. Broome, DSC, RN an old hand in Western Approaches and, incidentally, the author of the sketches in this book which originally enlivened the 'Bible' of the escort forces, the Western Approaches Convoy Instructions.

So the wheel had come full circle and I was back in the splendid ship which I had so sorrowfully left sixteen months before—and with every prospect of taking her into action.

CHAPTER 6

Huff-Duff

WHEN I rejoined *Hesperus* I found that the officers had all changed since I was last in command except for David Seeley, but many of the ratings were still serving in her.

My new First-Lieutenant and anti-submarine specialist was A. H. Williams, ex-merchant navy, inevitably 'Bill', though he was also known as 'Slogger' which gives an indication of his burly physique and forthright manner. *Hesperus* had been having a quiet time for many months, which did not suit Bill and I fancy he hoped that the change of captains would bring with it a change of luck. It was some months before his hopes came true but I am glad to say that before he left me for a command of his own we had one outstandingly successful and satisfying day together.

It was clear at once that the wardroom made a very happy team. David Seeley (Lieutenant the Hon D. P. Seeley) and Mr Pritchard (Torpedo Gunner) were the only two RN officers, the remainder being RNVR except for my engineer officer, Lieut.-Commander Anderson, an Australian RNR. The rest of the wardroom team was made up by Tony Edlin RNVR, a son of the comedian well-known in the days of my youth, 'Tubby' Edlin, and George Carlow, a wartime RNVR from Glasgow. Tony had inherited his father's diminutive stature and something of an artistic temperament. His effervescent nature, coupled with a passionate devotion to the Navy, made him a very pleasant shipmate and a most efficient young officer. George Carlow combined the canny good sense of his native city with a most un-Scottish gaiety, which was of immense importance to us all in the times of boredom and discomfort which make up so much of life at sea in wartime, between the infrequent moments of excitement and drama.

The summer months, never a favourite time for U-boats, owing to the long hours of daylight, were amazingly quiet. The convoys escorted by B2 Group (the group of which *Hesperus* was the leader) ploughed peacefully to and fro across the Atlantic with never a sight of a U-boat.

Some groups were not so successful and some ships continued to be lost, but the lure of the happy hunting-grounds off the American coasts prevented the battle in mid-Atlantic from reaching the fury it attained in the following year. The comparative paucity of U-boats on the convoy routes enabled a well-handled convoy to evade the submarines lying in wait for it, provided news of the threat was received in time. It was here that the U-boat tracking room at the Admiralty, under the direction of Rodger Winn (now a QC), was extraordinarily successful. Time and again information was passed out to convoys giving the position of U-boats with amazing accuracy—far greater than the originators themselves ever claimed for their estimates. I also found that H/F D/F, or 'Huff-Duff' as it was always known, had by now attained an efficiency, in trained hands, which could give reliable warning of a threat to a convoy. As it played such an important part in my later encounters with the U-boats I must explain briefly its uses and limitations.

H/F wireless transmissions do not, like transmissions of lower frequency, follow the curvature of the earth, but go out in a straight line. They thus form a tangent to the surface of the globe, so that a transmission from a ship cannot be intercepted directly by another ship beyond the horizon. If it were not for the fact that owing to the nature of the upper atmosphere these transmissions are reflected back to earth, H/F transmissions would only be receivable at visibility distance, which depends, of course, on the height of the transmitting and receiving aerials. When transmitted by a submarine and received by a destroyer, this distance would not be more than 15–20 miles. Transmissions so received were known as the 'ground-wave'.

Those transmissions which returned to earth after striking the ionosphere were known as the sky-wave and could be received at almost any range. The strength with which sky-wave transmissions are received is no indication of the distance apart of two stations, but to an experienced handler of the H/F D/F sets it was possible to distinguish between a ground-wave and a sky-wave. If one of the former were detected it was possible to say that the transmitter was inside twenty miles.

Furthermore, owing to the rigid rules under which the U-boats were working, which entailed a signal being made to HQ on sighting a convoy or before going into the attack, the form and nature of these signals had become familiar to our monitoring stations ashore which passed on the information to our ships at sea.

Provided therefore that the H/F D/F set was listening on the frequency selected by the U-boat, or provided there was a sufficient number of sets in the escort group to cover all the frequencies used by the U-boats, these reports would be intercepted and, if on the ground-wave, were an immediate indication that the convoy was being shadowed or attacked by a U-boat. As the bearing could also be obtained it was then possible to send an escort or an aircraft out to hunt for the U-boat in its estimated position and keep it down while the convoy steered a drastically new course. Even if the escorts failed to find the U-boat, and it was very much a needle in a haystack we were seeking, by the time the U-boat commander could again surface he would find an empty ocean with no indication of the direction in which his quarry had gone.

Such encounters with the enemy were frequent, but the reason that convoys escorted by B2 Group maintained such immunity I put down largely to the uncanny skill of the officer whose sole job in *Hesperus* was to operate the H/F D/F set. Lieutenant Harold Walker RNVR (known always to us as 'B-Bar' from the opening Morse symbol of the U-boats' signals) was an ex-Marconi operator who had not only spent two weeks in an open boat after being torpedoed in a merchant ship, but had suffered the loss of both his parents and his fiancée in air-raids. A passionate hatred for Germans kept him for long hours of the day and night brooding over his dials and conjuring out of the air vital information on the activities of the enemy. Time and again he gave warning of impending attack and we took suitable action to shepherd our charges away from the danger. He had also the useful faculty of being able to distinguish the touch on the Morse key of one operator from another and could recognise, for example, the peculiarities of a signal being transmitted on wet aerials and therefore probably by a U-boat just surfaced. All this combined to give us a tremendous advantage and his value to me can best be illustrated by the fact that the only loss of a ship from a convoy escorted by B2 Group took place when 'B-Bar', for once, failed to intercept the vital first-sighting report by a U-boat.

I was very glad that later in the campaign Harold Walker was awarded a Distinguished Service Cross, after having been twice mentioned in despatches.

Many were the ruses employed to shake off shadowing U-boats. One escort commander once organised a mock-battle after dark well clear of the convoy with the idea of drawing any U-boats in the vicinity into a wild-goose chase. Unfortunately, though the commodore of the convoy knew of the plan, he had not been able to pass it on to the ships of the convoy and, when star-shells and searchlights were seen in the distance, some over-eager ships took this to be a signal for firing the illuminating rockets known as Snowflakes, designed to turn night into day and expose any U-boat lurking between the columns. This ruse was not tried again.

I remember one voyage in which evasion tactics were particularly successful, and as it happens that both our main enemies were encountered, the U-boats and the Atlantic weather, the story of it may serve to typify a convoy voyage of that period.

On this occasion the convoy, a slow outward-bound one, ONS 138, sailed from Liverpool on the 11th October, 1942. It immediately ran into foul weather and before it could even be properly formed into its ocean formation, the ships, mostly in ballast and riding high out of the water, were scattered hopelessly. For days on end it was impossible to do much more than heave-to and avoid weather damage. In the brief intervals of slightly less savage conditions, the escorts managed to gather small parties of ships together but the next gale would then come roaring out of the west and, when visibility cleared again, the sheepdog work had to be begun all over again. So it went on for nearly a week until finally on the 18th the weather moderated sufficiently for the majority of the convoy to form up. Even so for the next three days the convoy made good only three knots. Already, with the journey hardly begun, fuel in the destroyers *Whitehall* and *Vanessa* was getting critically low and unless they were sent immediately to Punta Delgarda in the Azores, where we had fuelling facilities, or unless the weather moderated sufficiently for them to fuel at sea from the tanker accompanying us for that purpose, they would soon find themselves in the ignominious position of lying helpless in mid-ocean awaiting a tow. The decision had to be made—a constantly recurring one for any commander of a force at sea, to whom the fuel 'state' signalled in daily by his ships was always a matter of utmost importance. I felt that the savage weather could not go on much longer and decided to keep them with the convoy. For this run we were taking a route much further south than usual and it seemed that we must soon run into the blue weather and steady breeze of the trade winds. On the 21st October, Trafalgar Day, the hoped-for change came and, just in time, the escorts were able to top up their fuel tanks. With the sunshine drying us out and the convoy at last able to make its scheduled 7 knots, we felt in better heart to meet any threatened attack.

It was not until the evening of the 23rd, however, that the enemy gained contact with us. Soon after dark came the ring from 'B-Bar' in his D/F office to say he had intercepted a U-boat's sighting report astern of the convoy and fairly close. Taking *Vanessa* with me, we chased off down the bearing, hoping to pick up the U-boat on our radar before he dived; but he was too quick for us and we returned empty-handed.

Before we had got back to the convoy further signals were intercepted from other submarines and 'B-Bar', with his ability to distinguish one transmitter from another, identified four separate U-boats in contact with us. There were all the makings of an ugly concentration followed by a pack attack on the convoy, and steps had to be taken to keep the U-boats from travelling on the surface to their attack positions. Throughout that night *Hesperus* steamed at high speed to one after the other of the estimated positions of the U-boats. No contact was made but we hoped that we were keeping them down and spoiling their plans.

At daylight *Hesperus* rejoined the convoy and we awaited what the day would bring. We had not long to wait, for at 0830 the D/F office reported the U-boats chattering again, and now they were in a position of advantage, ahead of the convoy.

Once again, with *Whitehall* this time, *Hesperus* romped off to try to gain contact. The sight of smoke in the suspected direction gave us a momentary hope of success but to our dismay it soon turned out to be from a Greek ship which had never managed to rejoin the convoy after the gales and was now steaming along blissfully unaware of the U-boat probably even then stalking her. Why she was not torpedoed is a mystery, but perhaps the U-boat commander had never heard of the 'bird in the hand' and was waiting to get at the bigger target of the convoy. Shooing the Greek back into the fold we continued our search, but to no avail.

Then at about 1045, another bearing came up to the bridge, of a U-boat which we estimated to be on the port bow of the convoy. Off we dashed again. The weather was now the blue calm of the southern latitudes and crystal clear. A cry came from the look-out in the crow's nest up the mast. He had sighted an object on the horizon but could not see it clearly enough to identify it. At full speed we steered in its direction but, before we could get a clear view of it, it vanished. I felt sure it must have been a submarine which had dived, but in that extreme visibility the eye can play queer tricks on one. Another difficulty, supposing it were indeed a U-boat which had been seen, was to judge its distance, for a mirage can throw one's estimates hopelessly out. However we made our guess and on reaching the estimated position *Hesperus* started an asdic search. Much as I had longed for an easement of the weather I now began to curse the hot, calm day that was now on us. For it was the worst possible conditions for the asdic. Furthermore the sea was alive with shoals of fish, enjoying the warmth of the Gulf Stream and each one sent back an echo which had to be tested and listened to in case it might be from a submarine.

About midday we did get a contact which could be a submarine and I ran in and attacked it with depth-charges. As we prepared to attack again, once more the masthead lookout shouted down and this time he was sure it was a U-boat he could see. Things were getting hot and though it was dangerously denuding the convoy escort I felt it was vital to scotch this threat and ordered *Whitehall* and *Vanessa* to join us at full speed, while *Hesperus* went bald-headed for the U-boat we had sighted. Although we got to within four miles of it before it dived, the asdic conditions were hopeless. The only thing to do was to sweep the area and keep the U-boat down until the convoy had drawn ahead and clear.

By this time I was beginning to have a feeling of being surrounded by U-boats and was not at all happy about the prospects of the convoy in the coming night. Fortunately we were due to make a large alteration of course to the westward, having now come as far south as our planned route allowed for. If I could keep the U-boats down until dusk and then make the alteration of course, we might give them the slip.

With *Whitehall*, therefore, *Hesperus* spent the rest of the day sweeping the dangerous sectors, ahead and on the bows of the convoy. This kept the U-boats quiet until the evening, when once again they were heard, but to my relief out to the south of the convoy. We were getting them where we wanted them if the plan was to work.

Another idea to help us to evade was also working in my mind. We had as a passenger for the trip, Admiral Usborne, then retired from the Navy, but well known as an exponent of the use of smoke. I am not sure whether he first brought up the idea, but certainly the thin haze that was rising as the sun went down, was producing splendid conditions for the use of white smoke and I thought that, if we could lay a few banks of this artificial fog between the estimated positions of the U-boats and the convoy, it might help to bewilder them when they surfaced to resume their chase. So, asking the commodore to make his alteration of course when night was falling, I arranged for corvettes of the escort to lay smoke floats in suitable positions so that the smoke would lie between the estimated positions of the U-boats and the convoy, while the destroyers with their apparatus for making white smoke steamed up and down to lay a further cloud. I had not much faith in this ruse but, with asdic conditions so maddeningly bad, I felt that anything was worth trying. But there was one U-boat which, from wireless bearings, we had earlier plotted in a position in which we could not hope to deceive him, for he had been detected right in the path of the convoy. Unable to hunt him down, we could but hope that when the time came for him to manœuvre for an attack he would be forced to make some move that would betray his position.

All our escorts were very much keyed up and knew that dusk was likely to be the crucial time. I was very glad to get a signal from Lieut.-Commander Russell in *Gentian* that at 2000 she had gained an asdic contact close ahead of the convoy, followed by the sighting of a periscope.

There was no time for a planned attack. The U-boat had to be put deep quickly before it could get its torpedoes away. Russell very rightly rushed for the spot and plastered it with depth-charges just before the convoy arrived. He then had to wait with what patience he could muster while the columns of ships churned their way past, hopelessly disturbing the water so that until the wakes had disappeared there was little hope of regaining contact. As soon as they could, *Gentian* and *Vanessa* combed the area carefully and though they failed to gain contact they forced the U-boat to go deep and stay there, blind and immobilised, while the convoy moved ever further away on its new course towards its 'safe and timely arrival'.

Whether the other U-boats were deceived by our smoke-making I shall never know, but whatever the cause, as the night wore on we could hear their signals getting ever fainter and further astern till by morning we knew that we had given them the slip.

CHAPTER 7

The Showdown Delayed

AT this stage of the Battle of the Atlantic in the summer and autumn of 1942, a well-trained escort group had little to fear from the 'sea-wolves', although the enemy was quick to take advantage of any weakness or inefficiency of a convoy escort. Some convoys were severely mauled and suffered losses in double figures and in each case the escort was either, for some reason or other, weak in numbers, or it was composed of an inexperienced and under-trained team.

The majority of the latter came from the Royal Canadian Navy, and the succession of disasters which befell Canadian-escorted convoys at this period vividly illustrated the need for trained teams in the task of convoy defence. Individual skill and competence, of which the small pre-war Canadian Navy had plenty, were not enough. Unfortunately many of the ships manned by the Canadians were not given time even to acquire this before being thrown into the battle—with disastrous consequences.

The Canadians plunged into the war with all the zest and enthusiasm we have come to expect from this go-ahead people. Their Navy started the war with six destroyers and a total manpower of 2,000 men. But in their zeal to play a full part in the war, the RCN was expanded at a phenomenal rate. They built corvettes for themselves and some of the antiquated destroyers received from the Reserve of the US Navy in 1941 were taken over and manned by Canadians. By the end of the war the RCN had nearly 400 ships of minesweeper size or larger, and a manpower of nearly 90,000. This sudden expansion, however, inevitably meant that officers and men were going to sea with only the sketchiest training.

During 1941 the Atlantic along the east coast of Canada,

and the ports of Newfoundland, became populated with a motley collection of warships manned largely by landsmen whose homes were perhaps a thousand miles from the nearest sea. Discipline was weird and wonderful, equipment was ill-maintained and training in its use sadly lacking. These ships were units with which to make a show on the operations room maps, and perhaps to give a semblance of security to convoys which would have otherwise gone unescorted, but they were little more. I am a great admirer of Canada and the Canadian people but no account of the Atlantic battle would be complete without reference to the quality of some of the warships under whose escort merchant convoys often had to sail. The Canadian effort to produce a Navy and so to help their hard-pressed brothers in the RN and the USN was magnificent, but it would have been more valuable if quality rather than quantity had been the aim.

I remember in my *Walker* days sailing from Halifax with one of these Canadian ships. It was supposed to be trained for combat, but on the first day every form of communication broke down one after the other and when the battery of her portable signal lamp—her last link with the outside world—gave out and no replacement was available, I was unable even to tell her CO what I thought of him, which was perhaps as well.

The appearance of many of these travesties of warships was unbelievably dirty and unseamanlike, but all records in this respect were broken by one corvette which was sent to me at Argentia from the Canadian base at St John's for a 'shake-up', though this was not normally part of my duties. This ship arrived with 'We Want Leave' painted on the side of her superstructure and I was therefore only a little surprised when my staff anti-submarine officer, Lieut.-Commander Kidston, came back from a visit to her with a look of horror still on his face. He found that the ship's company's hammocks were left permanently slung on the mess-decks—'In case they got tired during the day,' said the captain. The majority of the senior petty officers had been sent off on leave, although the ship was supposed to be available for operations. A glance at her depth-charge armament showed that the charges were for the most part rusted in to their housings though kept primed and armed.

The first step was to get these weapons set to 'safe', a job undertaken with the utmost trepidation by my gunner. She was then sent to sea, with Kidston embarked, to do a little simple training. Proceedings opened with the ringing of the alarm bell to get the men to their Action Stations. This achieved only a brisk display of Abandon Ship Stations. They finished with the firing of one of the suspect depth-charges, which lived up to its appearance by exploding close under the ship's counter on impact with the water.

However, with guidance and informed instruction, two things inevitably in short supply in a suddenly expanded Service, this ship improved out of all recognition.

Very understandably, the RCN was determined that their ships should operate as soon as possible in purely Canadian formations. From the point of view of successful prosecution of the war at sea this was unfortunate. Canadian groups were not until a late stage of the war in a state of efficiency which enabled them to meet the U-boats on equal terms. Their communications were bad, their radar was less efficient than that fitted at the same time in British escorts and they lacked the excellent intensive training facilities which were available in the UK. On one occasion I took over the escort of a convoy from a Canadian group in thick fog which persisted for the next two days. My radar screen showed throughout this time a ship close astern of the convoy which was presumed to be a straggling merchant ship, but when the fog finally cleared it turned out to be one of the Canadian escort group which had not only not received any of the signalled orders from her leader to leave the convoy, but had failed to record on her radar screen the arrival of my group and the departure of his comrades.

Such a ship was hardly likely to be much of a menace to the enemy in a night attack. With such material it was folly to assume responsibility for the defence of valuable convoys. It would have been wiser if the Canadians had pocketed their pride and sailed their ships with experienced escort groups until they were themselves battle-worthy. The tale of losses speaks for itself. September, 1942: 9 ships torpedoed from a Canadian-escorted convoy. October, 1942: 7 from a convoy with mixed American and Canadian escort. November, 1942, 13 ships sunk, escort Canadian, and again in December, 13 ships sunk from one Canadian-escorted convoy.

In February and March, 1943, further heavy losses overtook convoys escorted by the Canadians, although at this very time the U-boats were receiving the hammering in the Atlantic which turned out to be their decisive defeat on the convoy routes. It is true that a few British-escorted convoys suffered heavily during this period, but whereas these were exceptions which only served to drive home the lesson that only good team-work and a high degree of training could achieve success, with the Canadians it was a melancholy fact that almost every voyage at this period was a tale of disaster and sunken merchant ships.

The sad part of it all was that, individually, many of the Canadian escort vessels had most skilful and gallant crews which, put into contact with the enemy in reasonable circumstances, achieved splendid successes. But too often lack of early appreciation of a threat allowed them to become involved in the confusion and mêlée of a massed wolf-pack attack. With ships in the convoy ablaze and sinking, with distress rockets arching up into the sky as a ship is torpedoed, with lifeboats and rafts of desperate survivors littering the ocean, a Captain is robbed of that atmosphere of careful search and undistracted investigation which is so vital to the detection of an enemy submarine.

Some splendid successes were indeed achieved by Canadian escort vessels in the Atlantic. In September, 1941, a beautifully co-ordinated hunt and attack by two newly-commissioned corvettes, *Chambly* and *Moosejaw*, resulted in the surrender and sinking of *U 501*.

In July, 1942, the Canadian destroyer *St Croix*, after a copybook hunt and attack with depth-charges sank another U-boat. In the same month *Skeena* and *Wetaskiwin* destroyed another. Perhaps the highest degree of fighting efficiency was shown by the Canadian destroyer *Assiniboine* in August, 1942, in a running fight with *U 210*. In spite of the twisting and turning course of such a fight and with a fire caused by enemy shells raging under her bridge, *Assiniboine's* guns repeatedly hit the U-boat, which was further damaged by ramming and finally sunk.

Too often, however, actions in which the Canadian escort groups were involved were tales of wild and confused fighting through nights made hideous by the glare of burning ships and the deadly explosions of torpedoes. The wolf-packs were driven off and many of the wolves had wounds to lick, but not before they had done their deadly work in the convoys.

Tales of the Battle of the Atlantic which have been published in fiction form give the impression that every passage of a convoy was a hard-fought battle and losses inevitable. Early in the battle this may have been not too great an exaggeration; but with the advent of radar and of H/F D/F, a well-trained escort group had the measure of the U-boats, which could only attack at very great risk to themselves. An indication of the immunity achieved is the fact that *Hesperus's* group during the time I was in command, a period of nearly two years, lost only two ships in convoy, and they were smartly avenged within twenty-four hours.

So, during the summer and autumn of 1942, we plied back and forth across the Atlantic without getting into action. Though boredom and monotony were a very real problem to contend with, yet no two trips were ever quite alike, and somehow there was always a feeling of gaiety in *Hesperus*, the happiest of ships. Convoys varied from the 'fast' 10-knotters composed of splendid 10,000 tonners or larger, to the slow, nominally 7-knot, convoys. The latter almost invariably had one or two slow crocks of doubtful reliability which were little better than floating coffins. The majority of these sailed under the Greek flag, though not all of them, and I became sure that there must be a special corner of Hell reserved for shipowners who would send men to sea in the North Atlantic winters in such ships. When all was well these convoys would spank along at a dashing 5 knots, but these occasions were rare. The convoy routes took us into far northern latitudes in the vicinity of Iceland where westerly gales are almost continuous for months on end, and westbound convoys would for days make little or no progress. The 'fixing' of the ship and the computation of the distance made good each day was a depressing business and an anxious one. For the fuel endurance of destroyers is not large and some time during the voyage it was essential to top-up fuel tanks from the tanker accompanying us for this purpose. But to accomplish this required conditions better than a gale. During one of these gales I remember one of my ship's company being swept overboard. The alarm was given at once and though it was quite out of the question to think of lowering a boat, I was able, with a searchlight trained on the poor fellow, to manœuvre the ship astern so as to bring him alongside. David Seeley, always to the fore in rescue operations, went over the side with a line round his waist to try to pull the man aboard. He succeeded in getting him halfway up the side but the dead weight was too much for him; the man slipped from his grasp and was not seen again.

On the east-bound run, though the wind and sea were usually astern of us, this put a strain on the ramshackle steering-gear of the coffin-ships and, as often as not, one or more would come to a halt and drop astern of the convoy to patch themselves up, while the signal would go up in the commodore's ship for a reduction of speed to allow the laggard to catch up again.

However, all this period of relative inactivity was helping to weld B2 Group into a well-trained team. The signals required under any set of circumstances between *Hesperus* and the remainder of the group became fewer and briefer, for all the COs knew what they were expected to do and would be off in the required direction at once without waiting for orders.

At this time the group consisted of the destroyers *Hesperus* (my ship) and *Vanessa* (Lieut. C. E. Sheen DSC, RN), and the Flower-Class corvettes *Gentian* (Lieut.-Commander H. N. Russell DSC, RNR), *Clematis* (Lieut.-Commander C. Morrison-Payne RNVR), *Heather* (Lieut. W. L. Turner RNR), *Campanula* (Lieut.-Commander B. A. Rogers, RD, RNR),

Mignonette (Lieut. H. H. Brown R.N.R.) and *Sweetbriar* (Lieut.-Commander J. W. Cooper RNR).

Homeward bound in November, amongst the steady stream of signals, weather forecasts, situation reports and suchlike pouring out to ships at sea, came a personal one for me from HQ at Liverpool, informing me that I had become the father of a son on Guy Fawkes' Day. I thereby beat 'Bill' Williams, who was also 'expecting', by a short head. The five knots progress of the convoy seemed more than usually unbearable to both of us after that, but our home port was reached in time for us to make a dash home to see the new arrivals before setting off again.

For the next homeward-bound convoy the group left Argentia late in December 1942 and we had loaded up with many of the good things, obtainable from American sources, for a belated Christmas. It is strange to think that one of the things I nearly always managed to bring back was a sack of onions, at that time the rarest of luxuries at home. On this occasion it was turkeys, of course, and, as every man-jack on board had one to bring home, it was a problem where to stow them. Eventually the chief bosun's mate, a man of infinite resource, arranged for them to go in various compartments up near the bows without, he assured me too much impairing our efficiency should we get into action. I was to remember this arrangement rather ruefully later in the voyage.

The passage of the convoy HX 219 followed its, by now, usual peaceful progress and we had passed that lonely outpost of Europe in the Atlantic, Rockall, and would be dividing up the convoy into sections according to the destinations of the ships on the next day, when an opportunity arose to get a crack at the enemy without having first to consider that bugbear 'the safe and timely arrival of the convoy'. On the afternoon of Boxing Day the well-known shrill of the bell from the H/F D/F office, which by some telepathic means I could invariably diagnose as urgent before the telephone message came through, brought me hurriedly to the bridge. A U-boat had just transmitted a message reporting the sighting of our convoy from a position astern of us, and as we had

THE AUTHOR

HMS *Hesperus* in her war paint

With her bows dangerously buckled, the *Hesperus* returns to port after ramming and sinking *U 357*

Some of our prisoners come ashore

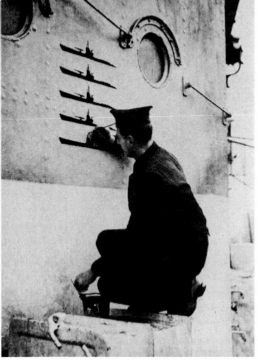

The *Hesperus*'s crew kept the score of U-boats sunk

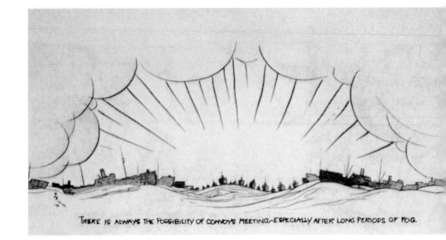

THERE IS ALWAYS THE POSSIBILITY OF CONVOYS MEETING—ESPECIALLY AFTER LONG PERIODS OF FOG.

Co-operation between our two Navies is essential

Two of the drawings by Commander 'Jackie' Broome
which enlivened the official Convoy Instructions

The Author (*right*) and his First-Lieutenant, Commander Ridley,
on the bridge of the *Bickerton*

The end of HMS *Bickerton*

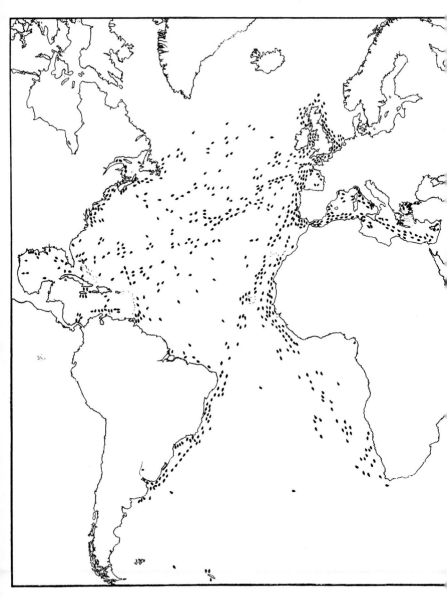

The distribution of British shipping in Home Waters, Atlantic and Mediterranean on an average day before the introduction of convoys

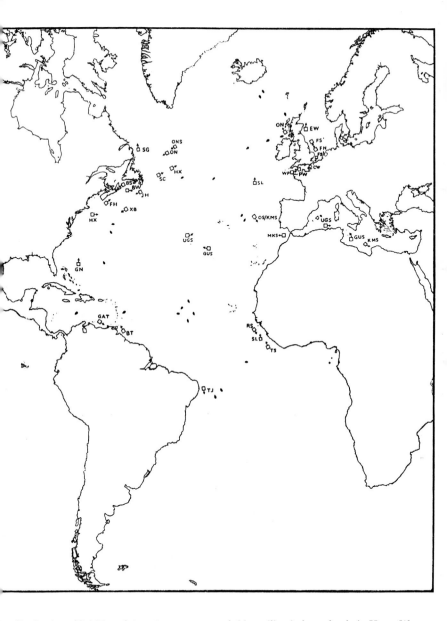

The distribution of British and American convoys and ships sailing independently in Home Waters, Atlantic and Mediterranean in mid-August 1943, when the convoy system was in full operation

received the ground-wave of his transmission, he was probably no more than ten to fifteen miles away. No need to worry about evasive tactics for the convoy or how to avoid the enemy building up a concentration of U-boats against us, for the convoy was nearly home and the U-boats at that stage were not operating near our coasts. A brief signal to *Vanessa* sent her galloping off on the bearing of the U-boat and, after a hurried signal to the Commodore to give him my intentions, *Hesperus* rushed off after *Vanessa*.

It was a sparkling winter day with a calm sea, except for the long Atlantic swell into which we were soon burying our nose, scooping green water up on to our forecastle and even on to the bridge. Only that morning, David Seeley, the horsey member of the wardroom, had remarked that it was a perfect day for the usual Boxing Day meet. Now we were off on a more exciting and deadly hunt.

As *Hesperus* punched her way into the swell, signals began to come in from *Vanessa*. 'U-boat in sight on surface. Bearing 235°.' Then: 'U-boat dived. Expect to reach diving position in 15 minutes.' Anxiously I wondered whether we should reach the scene of action in time to take part.

Vanessa, however, had failed to make contact with the submerged submarine and soon we joined her and I started to organise a combined hunt. We were going very slowly to allow *Vanessa* to take up station on us and were probing the depths with our asdic beam when I suddenly saw, to my astonishment, a full six feet of periscope rise out of the sea about fifty yards away. It was so close that I could see that it was trained steadily on *Vanessa*. It was so close, too, that it was impossible to turn *Hesperus* quickly enough to run over the U-boat to drop our depth-charges. Immediate action was vital for it seemed certain that such a bold U-boat had little respect for *Vanessa* and, thinking her to be alone, was shaping up to loose torpedoes at her. I yelled for 'full speed', tried to swing *Hesperus'* stern as nearly over the U-boat as possible and loosed a pattern of depth-charges, more with the idea of startling the U-boat and spoiling its captain's aim than in the hope of dealing it a fatal blow. With the explosion of our depth-charges the U-boat went deep and the hunt was on.

Very soon, as the confusion in the water from our depth-charge pattern died away, our asdic caught the U-boat in its sound beam and that most thrilling of sounds to a U-boat hunter, the answering 'ping' of an echo, came back to us. We ran in for our first steady attack. The shattering concussions of our charges and the upsurge of water from the depths seemed to indicate that the attack was delivered well and accurately. But though the U-boat must have been heavily shaken it was evidently not badly damaged for it remained below the surface and continued to manœuvre. *Vanessa* in her turn attacked with the same disappointing result. Water conditions for the sound beam were not too good. We were both having difficulty in holding contact and eventually what I feared took place. We both lost touch with our target. The asdic searched in a widening arc but no answering 'ping' came back. A hurried inspection was made of the mechanical plot on which were marked our own tracks and the calculated track of the submarine, and a combined search by the two ships was organised to cover all positions which the submarine could have reached.

The next half-hour was a desperately anxious time. Had the submarine given us the slip, after seeming so securely in the bag? Relations between 'Bill' Williams (who was the anti-submarine specialist officer as well as First-Lieutenant) and myself became almost strained, as each knew that if we had lost her the blame must surely lie somewhere between the two of us. But suddenly, when hope had begun to dim, an excited shout of 'Contact' came from the asdic operator and that blessed echo was back in our grateful ears. Once again we delivered our attacks but without apparent result. The short winter day was fading as *Vanessa* was called in to have another try while in *Hesperus* more depth-charges were being brought up from the magazine. It was not until darkness had fallen that the hammering we had given the U-boat bore fruit. A signal came from *Vanessa*: 'U-boat on surface. Am ramming.' But the enemy was not out for the count by any means.

He still had full speed on his diesel engines available and, in the darkness, he set off hell for leather with *Vanessa* in pursuit. The U-boat dodged and circled while *Vanessa* steered to ram. They actually came into collision at one time but *Vanessa* only managed to deliver a glancing blow and the U-boat, undamaged, set off again at full speed.

Gunnery against such a twisting eel-like target was useless and, indeed, we had to order *Vanessa* to cease fire as in the black night we were in as much danger as the U-boat of receiving her contribution.

Then *Hesperus* took up the chase. The U-boat turned and twisted. Every dodge I had ever learnt about ship-handling was brought into play to keep him ahead and in a position to be rammed or depth-charged. The engine room telegraphs clanged madly and in stokehold and engine room stokers and artificers worked like demons to keep the engines at full power. The ship shuddered in her bowels as an engine would be reversed in my efforts to claw her round inside the tighter turning circle of the U-boat. In the wheelhouse the coxswain swung the wheel desperately in answer to my stream of orders.

The end came with dramatic suddenness. The two signal searchlights on the bridge had been kept trained steadily on the conning-tower of the U-boat and they no doubt effectively blinded her captain so that he at last made a false move and, to my joy, was to be seen steaming across *Hesperus'* bow. One final helm order to my sweating coxswain and it was clear that we must hit the U-boat squarely amidships. At the last moment the engines were stopped to avoid overrunning and the order passed, so very rare in modern sea fights, 'Stand by to ram'. The enemy disappeared under the flare of the forecastle and with a deeply satisfying crunch the ship came to a standstill. Cut neatly in half, *U 357* sank at once, leaving only a spreading pool of oil and one or two shouting survivors.

A straggling cheer came up to the bridge from all parts of the ship. On the bridge, the reaction after the desperate excitement of the chase was terrific. Handshakes and congratulations all round were the order of the day. I remember particularly the excited congratulations from young Ensign James N. Cecil, US Navy, who had come with us from Argentia for his first sea trip in a fighting ship (he was a communications officer on the Admiral's staff). He had not expected to be in at the death of a U-boat on his first voyage.

But there was little time to sit back and congratulate ourselves. Two important tasks waited. To pick the few survivors out of the sea in the inky-black night, and to examine *Hesperus* below, assess the damage and shore up bulkheads so that we might safely get under way again. The first was successfully accomplished and a handful of dripping, battle-shocked Germans taken below. The report from the engineers took longer and was somewhat alarming. The ship's bottom for nearly a quarter of her length had been ripped out and compartments flooded. Until first-aid repairs could be made it would be unwise to put further strain on the ship's structure by going ahead. So there we lay, and even though it was unlikely that another U-boat would be in the vicinity, it is always a nervous business lying motionless, a sitting duck. But at last the temporary repairs were completed and we could go ahead and, though the buckled hull was no longer the sleek destroyer shape, we were soon able to work up to 15 knots.

It was at this stage that someone reminded me of our cargo of turkeys forward which were in the compartments well and truly flooded. A heap of oil-and-water-sodden corpses were all that remained of our hoped-for, belated Christmas dinners.

We were too elated at our success to mourn for long, however. By the morning we had overhauled the convoy and as we steamed up through the lines with a signal flying 'Submarine sunk', the ships gave us a noisy welcome on their sirens.

From our prisoners we learnt something of the tactics used by their captain, Lieutenant Kellner, who went down with his ship, in his efforts to avoid our attacks. Apparently he would wait until he heard us speeding up for the attack and would then make off at high speed. At the same time he would make drastic alterations in his depth. The number of attacks sustained without fatal damage was an indication of his success, but these tactics were inevitably a heavy drain on his battery power and on his supply of high-pressure air and would force him to surface very much sooner than if he had used less violent manœuvres. In the long run this was fatal to him. We also learnt that a device of which we had heard rumours had been used on several occasions during the hunt. This was a deception device known to the Germans as 'Pillenwerfer' and to us as a Submarine Bubble Target or SBT. This was a chemical bomb which effervesced on contact with water, thus leaving an area which returned the asdic's sound beam with a strong echo. The idea was a good one. An inexperienced asdic operator would hold on to this echo, much louder than, and perhaps masking, the echo from the U-boat, and before he had discovered his mistake the submarine would have moved off and might well escape. It was quite probable that our temporary loss of contact was due to our being led astray by this decoy.

Our arrival at Liverpool was a triumph. The late Captain 'Johnnie' Walker, our most famous and successful U-boat hunter, was having a brief period ashore at this time in charge of the escort base and he saw that we had a great welcome. As we steamed into Gladstone Dock, the crews of the other ships 'manned ship' and cheered us splendidly. Later the C-in-C, Admiral Sir Max Horton, who had taken over from Sir Percy Noble in November, 1942, came down to the ship to hear our story and congratulate the ship's company. Turkey or no, a very satisfactory leave followed for all, for with our damaged hull, a period in dry-dock was essential and there was no question of catching up with the next convoy cycle.

One sequel to this incident is amusing to look back upon and perhaps worth recording. The flooding of our fore compartments resulted in a quantity of fresh provisions being ruined and it was necessary, of course, to account for these on paper. But the busy little bees who checked our accounts ashore pounced with glee on some discrepancy revealed, and after the celebrations and shouting were over a solemn Board of Inquiry met to study the enormity of our crime. 'Bill' Williams, who as First-Lieutenant was supposed to have time to count up the spuds and tins of beef at intervals, managed to collect 'Their Lordships' Displeasure' as well as one of his several DSCs.

CHAPTER 8

Sea and Air

WHEN *Hesperus* was docked down in a dry-dock in Liverpool, it was clear that we were in for quite a time. The fore part of her keel had been folded back like a clumsily-opened tin of sardines. It was in fact over three months before she could sail again—a heavy price to pay for sinking a U-boat and, though occasions must arise when probably the only way to finish off a submarine quickly and prevent it from turning the tables by launching torpedoes is to ram, an order came out soon after this, discouraging this method of attack.

The order gained weight from the fate of the *Harvester*, commanded by my old friend, Commander 'Harry' Tait, in March, 1943. Harry, in the midst of a desperate convoy battle, had rammed and sunk *U 444* but, having perhaps too much momentum at the moment of collision, *Harvester* ran right over the submarine and badly damaged her own propellers and propeller shafts.

While frantic efforts were made to get temporary repairs made, *Harvester* lay stopped and helpless amidst a concentration of U-boats and one of them, *U 432*, inevitably took the opportunity to put a torpedo into such an easy target. *Harvester* went down with the majority of the ship's company including her captain. Though their deaths were quickly avenged by the French corvette, *Aconit*, which destroyed the U-boat responsible, it was a grievous loss of an experienced and skilful escort commander and a well-trained and efficient ship's company.

The question of what to do about a submarine which, though unable to dive, retained its mobility on the surface, remained a problem and I was to come up against it later. To stand off and engage such a small target by gunfire was to restore to the submarine much of the advantage it had lost, particularly when the Germans started to arm them with acoustic-homing torpedoes which would 'home' on to the sound waves from a ship's propellers and which needed to be aimed only approximately accurately to find their target. To counter these weapons, a device was produced known as the 'Foxer', which consisted of a pair of noise-makers towed some distance astern, which would attract the acoustic device of the torpedo and lead it astray. It was a cumbersome arrangement and we all hated using it. Although a simpler version with only one noise-maker—known as a CAT—became available later, the use of them reduced one's manœuvrability. Also the noise they made could be heard on the asdic so that the detection of an echo had to be achieved through the clattering of the noise-maker and greatly reduced the efficiency of the asdic operators.

It must be remembered also that ships of the escort forces had usually only very primitive gunnery control instruments and even the number of guns they carried had been reduced to make way for more depth-charges or other anti-submarine weapons.

While I was thus kicking my heels ashore, the Battle of the Atlantic was flaring up with a new intensity. The Germans, no longer finding the American coast the soft spot it had been, were concentrating their U-boats in mid-Atlantic. Their patrol lines were now so closely disposed that it became impossible for the convoys always to evade them.

The first U-boat to sight a convoy would whistle up the wolf-pack and the battle would be on. It was still possible, given highly-skilled operators on the H/F D/F and a fair measure of luck, to be warned of an impending attack in time, and so to manœuvre the convoy that the wolf-pack was given a stern chase.

If an air escort were present to prevent the U-boats from steaming on the surface, they would have only the shortening hours of darkness in which to circle round the convoy to an attacking position ahead. Of course, an even surer way of preventing a concentration of U-boats on a convoy was to sink, or at least force to remain submerged, the one which first sighted you.

Navigation from the conning-tower of a submarine heaving on an ocean swell is an inaccurate affair and to achieve a meeting with other U-boats it was usually necessary to 'home' them by radio. That is to say, one U-boat would transmit at intervals and the others would take bearings and adjust their course accordingly. But if the shadower were put down, the wolf-pack was left groping in the wide ocean spaces with only a doubtful navigational position calculated from the sighting signal to guide them.

But such tactics were not always possible and other escort group leaders did not have my wonderful 'B-Bar' in the H/F D/F office. They therefore found themselves occasionally heavily beset without prior warning and had to fight their way out of the wolf-pack encircling them. Convoy losses mounted steeply, but so also did the U-boat killings.

It was not until April, 1943, that *Hesperus* was ready for sea. While being repaired, she also gained a new acquisition in the shape of a 'Hedgehog'. This was a weapon which, mounted on the forecastle in place of A gun, could fire a pattern of twenty-four depth bombs 250 yards ahead of the ship on to the estimated position of a submarine. The bombs exploded on impact only, but a single hit on the hull of a submarine was calculated to be sufficient to tear a hole and so sink her. The fact that a near miss was literally 'as good as a mile', which was not so with a depth-charge, was a disadvantage, but we had long felt the need of a weapon of this sort which would enable us to deliver an attack while still in asdic contact. For with a depth-charge attack, in which it was necessary to run over the submarine, contact was lost as the ship got close and there was a 'dead period' during which the submarine could manœuvre away from its previously forecast position. We were all very excited about our new weapon and hoped to get a chance to use it.

As on this next trip I was to find myself co-operating with one of the new escort aircraft carriers, a few observations on the air aspect of convoy defence and the development of sea/ air co-operation are necessary.

Among the weapons at hand in the defence of our convoys and which steadily developed in efficiency as the war progressed, aircraft must be given an important place. By the beginning of 1943, convoys crossing the Atlantic could be assured of the sight and sound of aircraft in constant attendance except for a gap in the centre which was out of range of shore-based aircraft from either side of the ocean. Later, even this gap was covered by very-long-range aircraft (VLRs) and a further development, the conversion of merchant ships into small aircraft carriers (Merchant Aircraft Carriers or MAC ships), enabling a convoy to take its own defence with it, was put in hand in the autumn of 1942 and bore fruit the next spring.

But for a long time there was a considerable portion of every trans-Atlantic crossing where no aid from the air was available. The U-boats appreciated this and chose this area if possible for their operations. However, even in the areas close to our shores it is an unfortunate fact that the story of sea/air co-operation was not a happy one. Throughout history we can find examples to show how very difficult it is for any force to operate efficiently when there is divided control of any important weapon. Aircraft in maritime operations are no exception.

Coastal Command of the RAF had a poor start in the war owing to years of neglect, being then, as now, the Cinderella of the service. Except for a few torpedo-bomber squadrons, there was no glamour in Coastal Command. Maritime reconnaissance and patrol was a job of the utmost tedium. The training required was largely nautical, which suited only a small minority of those who chose the RAF as a career. Finally, inter-service jealousy prevented, until April, 1941, even the operational control of maritime aircraft being exercised by the command for whom they were supposed to be working.

The arrival of aircraft to aid in the defence of a convoy was not, therefore, always the happy event it should have been. The crews which manned them were usually quite out of touch with the Navy and hardly knew a merchant ship from a frigate.

The importance of quick and efficient signalling between aircraft and escorts was little understood and training in ship-air communications was sadly neglected. On many, many occasions, weary hours were spent trying to get important instructions through to Coastal Command aircraft, first by radio and then by signal lamp.

Often the struggle had to be abandoned and at other times a large proportion of the aircraft's time with the convoy was wasted in this unprofitable way, when a quick exchange of signals might have put the aircraft on to a submarine known to be shadowing the convoy.

A code of very brief signals was devised to cut down signalling to a minimum. A typical one was the signal IGO which meant, 'My time with the convoy is up, I am returning to base'. An example of the futility of some of the air patrols round the convoys and the lack of understanding of the tactics necessary, occurred on one occasion when the Sunderland flying boat which had been with us for some time, passed over the convoy and signalled, 'There is a U-boat shadowing the convoy from astern. IGO!'

Another example of the inefficiency prevailing at that time has been given me by Lieut.-Commander John Filleul, then First-Lieutenant of the sloop, *Starling*, commanded by Captain Walker. This account of his trip with Coastal Command is given in his own words:

At 3 p.m. on a Sunday afternoon the Captain came into the wardroom and asked if anyone would like to go for a joy-ride. As most of the bodies were half asleep, it being 3 p.m. on a Sunday afternoon, nobody answered. As I was Number One I felt rather responsible and to fill the gap asked where the joy-rider was to go from and to. The Captain then said it was to fly to Poole and then on the following day, to go for a trip over the Bay of Biscay to make contact with the Second Support Group.

My wife lived in Poole so straight away I said that I was very interested, and I duly set off.

Arrived at Poole Harbour, I was taken up to the Harbour Heights Hotel where I had stayed often before the war but which was now RAF Headquarters, and introduced to the Group-Captain. He suggested we should have a conference at 9.30 the following morning. I wondered what on earth we were going to confer about and I suppose my face showed some doubt because he then said 9.30 was obviously too early and 10 o'clock would be better. I agreed, said good night and went to see my wife.

The next morning I rolled up at 10 o'clock and for twenty minutes we all sat round a conference table talking about the weather and saying how wonderful it was to have such marvellous inter-service co-operation. Then it happened—had I got the orders?

'What orders?'

It then came out that they thought I was an officially appointed liaison officer fully briefed for the operation. I thought I was there for the joy-ride. By pure luck I had seen a long signal about the operation before I left Plymouth and was able to tell them a certain amount about it with the suggestion that they get hold of this signal. It was agreed to adjourn and wait until the signal could be got hold of.

Later in the afternoon we reassembled for a second go at the conference. They had the signal and asked me if it was the right one. In this signal were the alternative rendezvous positions for our meeting with the Second Support Group. The signal contained three latitudes but no longitudes. I said I really did think there were some longitudes and would it, perhaps, be worthwhile having another shot to try to get them? This was agreed. The conference was adjourned.

Two hours later we reassembled again and this time we had the complete signal and I tried to clear up any points that they did not understand. Everybody was happy. I was told: 'Alright, take-off will be at 2300 and you will brief before they take-off, won't you?'

I wondered how on earth one did brief air-crews and agreed. Just before 2300 I was ushered into the briefing room, which seemed to bulge with RAF, and was introduced by the Group-Captain. I had previously decided that as I hadn't the faintest idea how to brief an air-crew, the best thing that I could do was to give them a pep-talk. So I outlined the capabilities of our group which would be increased so much with their co-operation as they could be our 'eyes', and then told them that the five sloops could deliver a weight of attack of something like 750 depth-charges. I also drew their attention to the fact that they could only stay in an area for a matter of hours whilst we could remain there a fortnight. They seemed to be impressed with what I said.

Directly after this the crew and I were ferried out to a Catalina in Poole Bay and we prepared to take-off. Enthusiasm was running very high. In due course we dashed across the harbour and became airborne. Soon afterwards I noticed that there seemed to be a great desire by practically everyone on board to get into the same spot in the aircraft and naturally wondered why. I picked up a headset of the 'intercom' and heard the tail end of a conversation.

'Yes, I should think that there will be a hole a couple of feet square in a few minutes.'

I realised what had happened—in our enthusiasm to take-off no one had let go the moorings and the chain which attached the aircraft to a buoy was still with us and bashing up against the fuselage. The pilot decided we had better land in Poole again and get rid of this embarrassment and he called up Base to get them to switch on the flare path across the harbour again. Unfortunately, as far as Base was concerned we were airborne and they had lost interest in us.

He could make no contact so, as there was little choice, the pilot decided to press on for the Bay. Just before the fuselage was actually holed, one of the crew managed to get a boathook down through the flare shoot, grapple the chain and lash it with a piece of rope so that it stopped bashing us.

We flew through the dark hours towards the Bay. With dawn arrived a mist which cut visibility down to about a couple of miles. At this time there were often packs of six or eight JU 88s patrolling the Bay with the object of shooting down any Sunderlands or Catalinas which might be in the area and similar packs of our Mosquitoes were around trying to prevent this. JU 88s and Mosquitoes look very similar at a distance.

Suddenly the alarm klaxon sounded and we were told that an unidentified aircraft was approaching. Everyone dashed to their action stations. I tried to make myself scarce and keep out of the way, but was told that I was 'Blister Gunner' and was to man the point five machine-guns. This was interesting so I quickly asked one of the crew where the trigger was because this seemed a basic piece of information that I should have. On being told, I manned my weapon and hoped for the best. The aircraft turned out to be a Mosquito. I was very relieved.

After many fruitless hours looking for U-boats and the Second Support Group, with the odd alarms in between, we came across HMS *Hesperus* and her group. As we were not too sure where we were, it was decided to ask her for our position. We circled for nearly half an hour while *Hesperus* flashed an answer, each man in the aircraft reading what bit he could see and shouting it into the 'intercom'. Usually the navigator takes all this down on a pad. Then the pilot said:

'Alright, read it back.'

Absolutely nothing happened. No one had been taking it down! The pilot's remarks were, to put it mildly, unprintable. He decided he wouldn't go through the whole rigmarole again and that he would head in the general direction of England. He would probably hit some part of it. As it happened, we hit England just in the right place and landed in Poole Harbour as planned. We were de-briefed—a process of cross-questioning to get all available information out of the crew—and let loose. But not quite loose. The next aircraft was due to take off in about half an hour. Would I brief the crew, please. I did my best. My joy-ride had, after all, been an interesting experience.

But what a waste of manpower and material! That aircraft, with a properly-trained crew, could have been invaluable to some escort commander trying with inadequate resources to fend off a wolf-pack attack.

These same aircrews who showed such a lack of training for co-operation with the Navy, displayed the greatest dash and enthusiasm attacking U-boats when they could find them. In this there was glamour and excitement and very naturally the airmen were trained to a hair for it. But convoy escort seemed a dull and pedestrian job, though, given real co-operation with the warships, it need not always have been, and the airmen's hearts, with a few exceptions, were not in it.

Similar exchanges to get the two Services to know one another better were indeed arranged and one or two RAF officers who came to sea with me on convoy trips, showed great interest and no doubt were better versed in the requirements of sea/air co-operation on return to their units. In return I went over to the RAF Station, Limavady, in Northern Ireland, to take part in an anti-U-boat patrol in a Whitley aircraft. Unfortunately a convoy escort flight could not be arranged, but the patrol I took part in confirmed my fears that our Coastal Command aircrews of that time had much to learn before they could pull their weight in anti-U-boat warfare.

The first cause for concern was when the navigator reported that the bomb-sight in the nose of the aircraft had been wrongly assembled and was out of action for the trip. As this was required for finding the strength and direction of the wind, navigation after leaving the coast was very much a matter of guess-work. I then noticed that the only visual look-out kept was from the two cockpit seats through small square windows with a very limited field of vision. For the rest, look-out was confined to the screen of the radar set—which I noticed failed to register such objects as fishing boats which were sighted as we flew over them.

The bomb-aimer's position in the nose, with an almost all-round view, remained vacant until I got permission to occupy it myself. Furthermore I found that the only pair of binoculars in the aircraft were the pair of Zeiss, once the possession of Otto Kretschmer, which I had brought with me.

Perhaps the saddest part of this story was what took place subsequently. For errors such as these were only matters of training and experience which could easily be rectified, once discovered. But on return to Liverpool I was told to render a report, together with any lessons learnt, and this being addressed to my immediate superior, the Captain (D) Liverpool, I saw no reason to omit any of the shortcomings. I do not know how tactfully or otherwise these were conveyed to the people concerned, but inter-service feelings were outraged and umbrage taken. A lengthy correspondence was necessary to smooth ruffled feathers and to try to convey the idea that we were, after all, fighting the same battle and that my suggestions were given in good faith.

The Navy is constantly sniped at for wanting to take over the functions of Coastal Command, but who can blame her with the memory of the bitter experience of the last war still fresh in mind. Post-war experience with maritime reconnaissance and anti-submarine work by Coastal Command does not provide any evidence that things are any better today. It has always puzzled me that the RAF should hold on so doggedly to the right to control aircraft over the sea when at the same time they pay so little attention to the efficiency and equipment of Coastal Command. The latest bombers or fighters are constantly written up, discussed or reported in the Press, but who ever hears of Coastal Command's activity? It has no glamour and no role in atomic war, so it takes a back seat.

One of the arguments commonly used is that it was Coastal Command which 'turned the tide' in the Battle of the Atlantic and in support of this are usually given impressive figures of the number of U-boats sunk by the Command. The figures are correct but what is not pointed out is the fact that the majority of these successes were achieved after May, 1943, the month in which the Battle of the Atlantic was virtually won and Dönitz withdrew his forces from the convoys, admitting that the German Navy could no longer face the appalling losses they were suffering.

Coastal Command, or indeed maritime aircraft from any source, might very well have 'turned the tide' long before May, 1943, had the principle been understood that the place to win the Battle of the Atlantic was in the vicinity of the convoys. So far as surface escorts were concerned this had been appreciated as far back as 1941, but maritime aircraft, which might have been used to strengthen convoy escorts, were misemployed bombing the U-boat bases, *entirely without result* until the last stages of the war, and patrolling the U-boat transit areas. This latter tactic in the Bay of Biscay is often quoted as Coastal Command's major contribution to the winning of the Battle of the Atlantic. The facts are disillusioning.

Up to May, 1943, attacks on U-boats in that area had averaged only one success per month. In May, 1943, it rose to seven and in July when the defeated U-boat fleet was retreating helter-skelter to its bases, the number was fifteen. The total of Coastal Command successes contains a high proportion of 'kills' in the last stages of the war in German coastal waters and in harbour.

No; where Coastal Command played its most important role, in spite of the half-hearted way it often went about it, was *in the vicinity of convoys*. Untrained in co-operation with the Navy as our aircraft were, the remarkable fact is that only nineteen merchant ships out of the huge numbers sunk during the war, were lost when both air and surface escort were present. These figures were, of course, not available to us at the time, but we knew only too well what a colossal help air escort could be and it was all the more disappointing when for one reason or another the air contribution was inefficient.

It was therefore a very great step forward when the escort carriers began to come forward and naval aircraft, manned by crews properly trained for the job, could accompany convoys throughout their voyage or could be sent to aid an escort heavily beset.

The first of these ships, HMS *Audacity*, had a brief and tragic life, being sunk by a U-boat in December, 1941, with heavy loss of life when accompanying a homeward-bound Gibraltar convoy. But in her short career she amply demonstrated the value of this type of ship.

Her loss was due to an error of tactics in that, instead of remaining in the centre of the convoy where her own escorts could join the defensive screen and where from experience she was more or less immune from torpedo attack unless the U-boat came right in amongst the convoy columns, her captain elected to operate some twenty miles to one side of the convoy track.

This was fatal, being just where U-boats shadowing or preparing to attack would lurk—and the inevitable occurred. In spite of this bitter lesson it was always difficult to convince captains of aircraft carriers that the wise thing for them was to stay inside the convoy or to operate at least fifty miles away. The latter course involved a delay in getting the slow-flying Swordfish aircraft with which they were equipped, to the scene of action. The only objection to the former tactic was a sort of claustrophobia which was very understandable but unreasonable. The situation was made more difficult by the fact that the captains of the carriers were usually senior to the senior officer of the escort and could not be given orders as to where they were to station themselves. The matter was finally settled by an instruction from the C-in-C banning the fatal intermediate position but otherwise leaving the carrier captain a free choice.

Audacity, however, was not employed as were the later escort carriers, to help in the defence against U-boats. At the time of her appearance, the Gibraltar convoys were suffering severe losses from attacks by long-range Focke-Wulf Kondor aircraft and *Audacity* was equipped with fighters to cope with them.

On the transatlantic run, air attack was rarely a serious menace but the long-range Focke-Wulf aircraft were sent out to search for our convoys and, having found them, would 'home' U-boats to the position. Thus one would have the maddening experience of seeing the black dot of a Focke-Wulf endlessly circling the convoy on the horizon and quite immune from anything we could do. The story goes that on one occasion the captain of an escort signalled to the German to ask him to go round the other way as he was getting giddy watching him. The signal was acknowledged and the German airman complied! To combat these nuisances, the first device was the fitting to certain merchant ships of a catapult from which was launched a Hurricane aircraft.

Once launched, the pilot had either to make his attack and then head for land, if it were within his very limited flying range, or otherwise to bale out and hope to be picked up by an escort. They were very gallant fellows who manned these aircraft, for the Atlantic is rarely the place to choose to alight in a parachute.

To add to their danger, on one occasion when I saw one of these aircraft launched, the sheet of flame which came from the catapult caused the other merchant ships to think that the aircraft they saw streaking past was an enemy who had just attacked the ship and they promptly opened fire, fortunately without effect.

Another development, this time for defence against the U-boats, was the Merchant Aircraft Carriers or MAC ships, which were merchant ships, mostly grain carriers, with a small flight-deck superimposed. There was no room for a hangar as they continued to carry their cargo of grain, so the three or four Swordfish aircraft they carried remained exposed to the elements throughout the voyage. It says much for the famous old 'string bags' that they rarely failed to get into the air when wanted. Though these ships did not get to sea until the summer of 1943, after the Battle of the Atlantic had been won, they were able to demonstrate how immensely they might have influenced the battle if produced sooner.

However, during 1942, the proper escort carriers, larger and with a hangar which could accommodate two squadrons of aircraft, were coming to sea, and they were first used with the Russian convoys. Then came a call for them to provide local air cover during the North African landings in October. It was thus not until early in 1943 that they became available to operate with the Atlantic convoys.

One of the first to be so employed was HMS *Biter*. She was commanded by my old flight-commander of the early days of the Fleet Air Arm, Captain Conolly Abel-Smith (now Vice-Admiral Sir Conolly Abel-Smith, Flag Officer, Commanding the Royal Yachts). I remember him as a most forceful and vigorous flight-commander who played as hard off duty as he worked in duty hours and we young pilots were expected to follow him in both activities, and great fun it all was. Conolly had been sunk in *Courageous* by a submarine when he was executive officer of that ship, so he had a score to settle with the U-boats and with *Biter* he soon succeeded in doing so.

CHAPTER 9

The Sinking of *U 191*

At last in April, 1943, *Hesperus* was ready for sea. Armed with her new Hedgehog and with the most up-to-date radar, we sailed on the 14th with Convoy ONS 4.

Besides our new equipment we had big changes in our ship's company. Many of the ratings had left to take their experience to newly-commissioned ships, to leaven the dough of wartime ship's companies.

Of the wardroom, 'Bill' Williams had left to take over command of the destroyer *Bulldog* in which he bagged another U-boat in due course. In his place had joined Lieut.-Commander Bill Ridley (now Commander E. W. Ridley DSC and two bars), who was to stay with me until August, 1944, and take part in several exciting battles.

Another addition was a Navigating Officer, Lyulph Stanley (Lieutenant the Hon. Lyulph Stanley RNVR), who also was to stay with me for the rest of my sea-going career in the war. Lyulph joined *Hesperus* shortly before we sailed and, on arriving in the wardroom and announcing he was the new navigator, was greeted by the brief statement, 'Bad luck, old boy. The captain eats navigators for breakfast'. This was an exaggeration and did nothing to give confidence to Lyulph when presented to me, the captain of his first ship, as a fully-fledged specialist navigator. But he need not have worried, for Lyulph, apart from being a splendid navigator and an utterly reliable staff officer, brought with him a charm of manner and a witty and scurrilous tongue which did much to enliven an already happy set of officers.

A new ship's company as well as new weapons meant that time was needed to reach efficiency. But, though before sailing the group was able to spend a couple of days undergoing tactical exercises with the organisation centred upon

HMS *Philante* (Tom Sopwith's yacht) at Larne, very little time was available to master the intricacies of the new gadgets. This was very nearly the cause of a serious failure on the trip which was in front of us.

The N in the convoy's code-number ONS 4 indicated that its route would be a northerly one and I knew that, even with spring on its way, this meant a fair share of gales and general dirty weather. How very right I was. As we 'climbed' inch by inch up the chart towards the Arctic circle the barograph in my cabin made its usual steep dive and, by the 17th, when our ordered route at last turned westward, a full gale was blowing. The convoy was almost stopped.

In the escorts water sloshed about the mess-decks and the wardroom. We were all cold and wet. In fact we were well and truly back in the North Atlantic, which Kipling immortalised with his poem about 50 North and 40 West in which 'the ship goes "wop" with a wiggle between and the steward falls into the soup tureen'.

For the next three days we just hung on and hoped for better times. Meanwhile *Whitehall* had gone ahead to Reykjavik in Iceland to pick up a few ships which were somehow to join up with us in mid-ocean where we lay in a welter of spray, of mountainous waves and scudding low clouds. Timely rendezvous in such conditions was a matter of pure luck against huge odds and HQ had passed a signal to *Whitehall* telling her to return with her convoy to Iceland unless in touch with us. *Whitehall* was still trying, unsuccessfully, to decipher it, when the longed-for break in the weather occurred and, to my immense relief, the two convoys hove in sight of one another.

In spite of the weather, U-boats had discovered the Iceland portion of the convoy and in heavy seas *Whitehall* had a brief but inclusive encounter with one.

Soon after the junction a signal came in from the Liberator aircraft attached to the convoy that she had sighted and attacked a U-boat. The incident is typical of many which, given efficient co-operation between ships and aircraft, could have resulted in a U-boat destroyed but as it was ended in failure and frustration. For the aircraft reported the position in latitude and longitude and it depended for its accuracy on the accuracy of the aircraft's navigation. Had the airman given the position relative to the convoy, an escort could have been with him quickly and a combined hunt might well have brought success. As it was, when *Whitehall* was sent racing off to where we estimated the aircraft's position to be, no aircraft was to be seen and as no radio communication could be established with the aircraft there was nothing for it but to recall *Whitehall* to the convoy. How we prayed for a little intelligent training to be given to these Coastal Command aircrews to match their enthusiasm and courage.

The next problem, as always on these occasions, was to refuel the two destroyers of the escort, *Hesperus* and *Whitehall*, for neither had the endurance to complete a transatlantic escort without refuelling. For it must be remembered that escorts must zigzag continuously at probably twice the speed of the convoy apart from high-speed forays to hunt suspected U-boats, to round up stragglers, or the thousand and one duties of escort. All this drinks up fuel.

To solve the problem the technique of fuelling at sea was perfected, at first by means of a floating hose towed astern of a tanker and picked up by the warship and connected to her fuelling system. This method, though at first sight simple and safe to employ in rough weather, suffered from unexpected difficulties and it was superseded later by the 'trough' method, in which the warship steamed alongside the tanker and hoses were rigged with loops in them so that, if the two ships surged apart, there was sufficient scope not to part the hoses.

It was never a manœuvre that I learnt to take lightheartedly in a seaway. The tanker from which one was to fuel would be rolling ponderously in the Atlantic rollers. The destroyer or frigate would be performing its lively antics, pitching and rolling in a corkscrew motion as one steered to edge gradually alongside. A suction abreast the stern of the oiler was caused by the displacement of water as she thrust her way through the sea and the water closed again behind her. This could suddenly swing one's bow inwards if one approached from astern, so it was wiser to converge on the tanker from abeam of her and turn up parallel when the distance between the two ships was right.

As the destroyer draws nearer to the tanker, the speed has to be adjusted with extreme accuracy and down in the engine room, knowing the importance of this, the artificers on the manœuvring valves stand with their eyes glued to the revolution counters. The revolution telegraph tinkles, calling for three revolutions per minute more and the valves are inched open with infinite care to comply.

At the right moment, on the upper deck, the line-throwing gun cracks and a line goes soaring over the tanker's decks to be quickly grabbed by her crew, bent on to a hawser which in turn is hauled back into the destroyer, bringing with it the end of the hose.

As the two ships get closer, their mastheads swinging in giddy arcs towards and away from one another, the seas heave and foam between them. Close enough now for safety, course is altered outwards a degree or two and the ships lie parallel and steaming at the same speed. A line marked with bits of coloured bunting is passed from one bridge to the other, helping the eye to judge the distance apart.

Meanwhile, in the tanker a derrick swings out, carrying the oil hose in a large bight or loop. This bight allows a certain amount of variation in the distance apart without bringing a strain on the hose. If the distance increases the loop is lowered from the derrick a little. As the ships draw together again the bight is hoisted up once more.

On the bridge of the destroyer, the distance apart and the relative speeds of the two ships require unwinking vigilance and, in a seaway, instant action is often needed to prevent any sudden variation from causing a collision or a burst oil hose with all the consequences of delay and unholy mess.

Oiling may take an hour or more and to ease the strain the captain often delegates the regulation of speed to another officer while he himself watches the distance apart and gives the necessary orders to the coxswain at the wheel to keep it right.

Perhaps the destroyer has been heavily engaged and is

short of depth-charges. These, too, can often be supplied by the tanker, and while one party attends to the oil hose, another hauls in the heavy canisters as they are hoisted over, and strikes them down into the magazine.

At last the moment arrives when the engineer officer signals for the tanker to stop pumping. Our tanks are full again. Quickly the hose is disconnected and hauled back into the tanker. With a shout of thanks to the master of the oiler and a few 'wisecracks' from one crew to the other, the destroyer draws away and shoots off in a cloud of spray to its allotted station on the escort screen.

With practice this could be successfully accomplished in surprisingly heavy weather, but there were limits and, if the Atlantic were in a vicious mood, day after day would go by while fuel got lower in the tanks and COs developed duodenal ulcers thinking of what would happen if the weather did not moderate.

But all was well in our case and in the next two days, while the convoy at last began to make westing and U-boats left us alone, the escorts refuelled and were again ready for anything. This was a relief, for, by the 22nd, we were entering that middle portion of the North Atlantic out of range of shore-based aircraft which the U-boats favoured.

On this occasion, however, they were in for a surprise, for drawing near us in support was the first of the larger escort carriers, HMS *Biter*, and her screen of four destroyers. By this time Harold Walker in his H/F D/F office was picking up a stream of W/T traffic from U-boats which made it clear that we were approaching a U-boat patrol line, and in the afternoon of the next day, Good Friday, 23rd April, his excited voice came over the phone to me: 'Enemy sighting report just been made. Very close—within ten miles. First class bearing.' Calling for the nearest corvette, *Clematis*, to follow at her slower speed, I turned *Hesperus* at full speed to the direction of the U-boat's signal. Within a few moments white spray surrounding a black dot could be seen on the horizon. A U-boat for sure! As its captain saw us racing for him, he crash-dived. But we had his position fairly well pin-pointed. Reducing speed, I set the asdic team to search the depths with their sound beam. 'Ping', 'Ping', the note went out. No echoes. Have we missed him? No! There it is. An echo firm and clear and we are in firm contact.

Here was a chance to try out our new killer, the Hedgehog. With Bill Ridley controlling the asdic team and a steady stream of bearings and ranges coming in I conned *Hesperus* slowly into the firing range. Everything was going perfectly. Conditions were good. Contact remained firm as we crept slowly into firing range. Then Bill Ridley's voice—'Fire!' It is with a feeling of shame that I have to record that nothing happened! A hasty check with the crew of the Hedgehog revealed what had happened. Unfamiliar with our new weapon, it had not been realised that the Hedgehog bombs, which had a complicated set of safety-pins to be removed one by one, would take so long to prepare. With twenty-four bombs to arm this took some time, and the crew had not had time, between 'contact' and the order to fire, to complete the operation. Quite rightly they did not obey the order. Our practice firings had been done with dummy bombs which were not fitted with the same safety device and so this time lag had gone unrealised.

Now we had to get this U-boat at all costs or we would never live down our shame. Fortunately, asdic conditions were perfect and, though the U-boat had evidently gone deep as usual, we were able to hold contact and deliver accurate depth-charge attacks. At one time during the action the asdic operators were led astray by the U-boat's use of SBTs (described in a previous chapter). But we were always on the look-out for this decoy device and in this case Bill Ridley quickly spotted the ruse and got the operator back on to the proper target.

By now *Clematis* had joined in the fray and also got in an attack. Then we ran in again and, together with the ordinary depth-charges, we loosed on the hapless U-boat another new weapon, a one-ton depth-charge. This was virtually a torpedo without engines, with its body filled with explosive and fired from our torpedo tubes.

After this, strange noises began to be heard on the asdic, like those made by a submarine surfacing. Excitement was intense and we expected at any moment to see the U-boat break surface. It was obviously shallower, and the chance had come to use the Hedgehog again. Once more we ran slowly in and this time, at the order, the twenty-four bombs went sailing away through the air to land with a splash ahead of us.

Nobody even whispered as we waited in an agony of suspense as the bombs dived down towards their target. Never have there been such long-drawn-out seconds as the hand crept round the face of the stop-watch. Suddenly two sharp explosions thudded through the ship. 'Got him, by God!' yelled Bill, as he popped up out of the asdic control cabinet, his face shining with excitement. And indeed we had. Gaping holes torn in her hull, *U 191* plunged to the bottom with all hands.

It was clear that we had put out of action the 'first sighter' of that particular patrol line of U-boats for the H/F D/F was soon able to report that no more were in contact. Of course, by now we had the inestimable benefit of having *Biter's* Swordfish patrolling on the horizon and, though for the next two days they made no sightings, while the convoy steamed on unmolested, we had the happy knowledge that should a U-boat be detected again by our H/F D/F, an aircraft could be directed on to him even more quickly than my 30-knot *Hesperus* could get to the spot. On Easter Sunday this very thing happened, not near the convoy but in the vicinity of *Biter* which was operating its aircraft some thirty miles away. The familiar sighting signal was heard on the H/F D/F and a bearing obtained. A warning was quickly radioed to *Biter* and shortly afterwards one of her patrolling Swordfish sighted the U-boat.

The submarine dived too soon for the aircraft to be able to get in an attack, but one of *Biter's* escorting destroyers, *Pathfinder* (Commander Gibbs), called to the area, quickly got contact and as quickly sent the U-boat (*U 203*) to the bottom. This was sea/air co-operation as it should be, and made us realise what could be done with properly trained aircraft.

On the following day the time had come for *Biter's*

group to leave us and, in her place to support us, was approaching a group of frigates, the 1st Escort Group under the command of Captain Godfrey Brewer. Brewer had been a destroyer man most of his career and was a friend of mine of long standing. Indeed we had first met when at the same preparatory school, so I was very happy to know we were to work together. His arrival coincided with fresh activity from the U-boats who had, as we thought, at last found our convoy again.

Once again the watchful 'B-Bar' had intercepted an enemy sighting report and *Whitehall* was sent racing down the bearing in the hope of repeating our success of Good Friday. He had not gone far, however, when Commander Bell found to his surprise the 1st Escort Group approaching from that direction. Evidently it was these ships that the U-boat was reporting.

He had not lingered on the surface and a search by the 1st Escort Group achieved no success but, from further signals intercepted, it became clear that the U-boat had followed the support group in and had taken up a shadowing position by nightfall. He could be heard calling his HQ at intervals and trying to get his report through over and over again, until finally Walker came to me and suggested a little ruse. Knowing intimately the German wireless procedure, he proposed that he should pretend to be another German unit, answer the U-boat and accept his message for onward transmission. This was a highly irregular proceeding, of course, but it seemed too good an opportunity of employing a little deception and pulling the Teutonic leg to be missed. I gave Walker permission to go ahead.

Soon afterwards he came to the bridge, all smiles, and reported that his 'dodge' had worked perfectly. The U-boat had stopped signalling, no doubt happily confident that Admiral Dönitz was massing a wolf-pack to his support. The U-boat commander must have been disappointed when nothing happened. While he waited vainly for his comrades to join him, we were able to give him the slip by making a big alteration of course after dark.

I have often wondered whether this U-boat commander

ever got home again and, if so, how he explained his apparent failure to report. But perhaps he was one of the many who failed to return from patrol in those spring months of 1943 when the U-boat attack was defeated with such heavy losses.

Meanwhile, free of menace by the enemy, the convoy found new hazards to face, for by the 29th, it was steaming through a sea studded with icebergs large and small. It horrified me to think of that great mass of shipping steaming blindly in the night through such a concentration of bergs, any one of which could rip the side out of a ship and send her to the bottom as efficiently as any torpedo.

We did what we could by illuminating with our searchlights the bergs in the convoy's path but for every large berg that we could detect on our radar there were dozens of small 'growlers' with their tops just breaking the surface. Amazingly, the columns of ships threaded the maze without disaster and on the following day we were nearing Newfoundland and could turn our charges over to the relieving Canadian escort group who were to take the convoy on to Halifax, Nova Scotia.

CHAPTER 10

Atlantic Bases

IT had been the longest Atlantic crossing I had experienced —sixteen days for a normally ten-day voyage, but our far-northerly route and the foul weather had set us back. It was with more than the usual sense of thankfulness that I 'rang off' the engines when *Hesperus* reached her berth at Argentia.

The first night in harbour after these voyages will always be highlighted in my memory. After the long, anxious days at sea in all weathers it was an unforgettable joy to be able to come aft to one's harbour cabin, to slough off one's clothes for the first time for many days and lie wallowing in a hot bath.

The clink of glasses would draw one to the wardroom later, where tongues were loosened by the unaccustomed 'noggins' which spread a happy glow through us all. It made up for all the wet and the cold, the long hours huddled in duffels, straining to see through the spray and the darkness, while the convoy crept snail-like across the ocean. In the little ships of the escort forces it was the weather that occupied our minds far more than the enemy.

The enemy we knew we could cope with, but the vindictive savagery of the Atlantic gales and the mountainous waves they raised, which came snoring down the wind at us, towering high above our heads, many a time put the fear of God into me. It was an almost tangible joy, therefore, to be snug in harbour in a secure berth, with a westerly gale moaning through the rigging, and knowing that an undisturbed night in one's bunk and between sheets lay ahead.

Probably the captain of a ship felt the reaction even more

than others, for at sea he was restricted to the bridge and the tiny sea-cabin and charthouse beneath it, taking his meals alone and rarely able to 'unbutton' with his officers.

Argentia, so far as we were concerned, was an all-male society and life often took a fairly noisy and riotous form. American officers would come on board to visit us from their 'dry' ships and occasionally some would be a little uncertain the next day as to how they got back to their cabins. Return parties would take place at the American officers' club and were equally hilarious. *Hesperus* parties invariably included the singing of a song we had adopted as our own—Lord knows where it originated—known as Zumba Za. It was sung entirely in German and represented a party of people each of whom in turn claimed to be able to play some musical instrument which he proceeded to do in mime, making the appropriate noises and gestures which were then taken up by the assembled party.

It started and ended with the double-bass whose notes were represented by Zumba Zumba Za—hence the name of the song. Somehow this apparently very childish entertainment always succeeded in being an enormous success, and it was invariably called for when the *Hesperus* officers were out 'on the tiles'.

Occasionally our 'turn-round' port would be St John's, which, being the capital city of Newfoundland, offered more sophisticated entertainment and female company. Some of the chief attractions there were the shops, all stocked with goods unobtainable at home. Most of us had lists from our wives or girl friends on the off-chance that we should get to this 'land flowing with milk and honey'.

I remember enlisting the aid of Lady Walwyn, the wife of Newfoundland's Governor, Admiral Sir Humphrey Walwyn, to choose baby clothes for my young son at home. She was a splendid shopper and the things were given a rapturous welcome by my wife. The irrepressible Jackie Cooper of *Sweetbriar* had been briefed to get scanties for his wife and nothing would satisfy him unless he had seen them modelled by the giggling 'Newfie' shopgirls, whom he quizzed through his monocle with a critical eye and a solemn face.

Wherever we did get into harbour, whether it was at Argentia or St John's, or back in our home base at Liverpool, *Hesperus*' group managed very successfully to forget the hazards of battle and storm and there was an amazing fund of good fellowship not only in individual ships but between the ships of the group which made us all into a well-knit team. The ship's companies were vastly proud of their group and its reputation for getting convoy after convoy across the ocean intact, while other convoys were suffering heavy losses.

It was hardly ever necessary to punish wrongdoers in *Hesperus*. All that was required was to let the culprit know that he would be drafted away from the ship if he could not reform and nearly always this was enough. Occasionally we carried out our threat and the rest of the ship's company were the happier for their loss.

In the wardroom I was always glad that so many officers from other ships of the group found pleasure in visiting *Hesperus*. The wardroom of the leader of a flotilla is not always a Mecca for officers from the other ships, but my staff had the happy knack of inspiring enthusiasm and affection.

Bill Ridley with his untiring craving to get to grips with the U-boats, and Lyulph Stanley with his irrepressible gaiety and capacity for fun, led the way and the others did not lag far behind. When the devil was in them they were no respecters of persons.

On one occasion in Liverpool when certain civilians in reserved jobs ashore were paying their customary visits to *Hesperus* for a little duty-free gin, Lyulph announced that he had got permission for them to come with us on our next convoy trip. He then sat back with a malicious grin on his face as 'they all with one accord began to make excuse'. There was, of course, no truth whatever in Lyulph's statement.

Another time in St John's, on a quiet summer evening, when the few officers remaining on board were gossiping over their evening glass of gin, Lyulph, who was Officer of the Day, was called forth by the quartermaster and informed in shocked Presbyterian, Scottish accents that there were nuns on the quarter deck. Even Lyulph was momentarily taken aback by this bold statement. As he told me afterwards it was one of the few emergencies not catered for in his training in HMS *King Alfred*, the school for budding RNVR officers. 'What do they want?' he asked. 'To see the Officer of the Day,' was the inexorable reply from the quartermaster who wanted no part in this popish plot. There was nothing for it but to get up on deck and find out what it was all about.

There they were, in their flowing grey robes, looking absurdly out of place on the deck of a warship. Saluting them courteously, Lyulph inquired their business, to be told they were collecting for charity. 'But, of course,' said Lyulph. 'Then you must come down to the wardroom and start with the officers.'

He could already visualise the expressions on the faces of his brother officers as he ushered two nuns into the wardroom. The nuns followed him down the steep iron ladder which presented no problem to them, negotiating it as if they had served for years in destroyers. 'Gentlemen,' announced Lyulph, 'these two ladies are here on a charitable mission and I am sure you will all be happy to contribute to their cause.'

The looks of blank astonishment that greeted this announcement were all that Lyulph could have wished for. But in no time at all the normal machinery of naval hospitality clicked into gear. 'What would you care to drink?' someone asked. 'Oh, we never take alcohol,' was the reply. 'Then perhaps a Coca Cola?' These were duly brought, but in their unescorted passage from the bar to the table, they were torpedoed by a large shot of gin. Perhaps it was the steward anxious to see a bit of fun on a dull evening in harbour.

Whoever it was, after two 'Cokes' the ladies began to behave most strangely. They talked, they laughed, they giggled and they stayed. Dinner-time came and went but the artless prattle of the nuns never ceased for a moment. When they finally realised the lateness of the hour there was a great flurry of robes and bobbing of wimples as they gathered themselves together and sailed up the iron ladder quite undismayed.

The buzz had got round the ship that there were 'queer goings on' in the wardroom and when the nuns reached the upper deck it seemed as though the whole duty watch was lining the side to see them off. But the nuns were magnificent. With a look of set determination, they marched down the gangway and, as their grey robes faded into the evening mist, their happy giggles floated back. All very reprehensible, but it was fun and no harm done and soon the authors of the prank would be standing their watch in an Atlantic gale, so who shall blame them?

The backing that the escort groups received at their base ports must be recorded in any account of the Battle of the Atlantic. Without it we could not have functioned efficiently and if it had been less thorough or less understanding of our needs we should not have been able to have that complete relaxation between trips that enabled us to go back to sea refreshed and eager.

The Western Approaches escort force was divided between several ports—Liverpool, Greenock, and Londonderry, and later also Belfast. I can only speak with knowledge of Liverpool for most of the war and of Belfast during 1944. The other ports may not have been so good—if they were better I would be astonished. Liverpool itself got off to a bad start and when I first knew it in 1940 it had nothing to recommend it.

A base staff of 'dug-outs' had no comprehension of the needs of ship's companies coming into harbour after sleepless nights and watchful days, longing for nothing so much as sleep, untroubled by the incessant need for precautions against wind and weather. There was no restfulness in a destroyer left to ride at her very light anchor gear in the 7-knot current of the Mersey and a full gale, when a little more careful organisation could have got her safely to a berth alongside and out of the tideway.

But such things are perhaps inevitable in the early stages of a war. They were certainly in marked contrast to the arrangements which held good later. A succession of experienced escort commanders held the appointment of Captain (D) Liverpool, the title under which went the officer in charge of the escort base. Captains Godfrey Brewer, 'Johnnie' Walker and Jackie Broome each held the job for a period and under their sway it was a wonderful experience to see the gates of Gladstone Dock close behind one's ship and to be taken competently in hand by a team of specialists determined to spare no trouble to have us 100 per cent efficient by the time our next convoy was ready.

In Liverpool, of course, we had the great advantage of being within a few minutes of the HQ of Western Approaches in Derby House where a brilliant organisation had been built up by Sir Percy Noble and his Chief of Staff, Commodore Jack Mansfield, and carried on by Sir Max Horton and his Chief of Staff, my cousin, Ian Macintyre. It was always a tonic to go to Derby House where one found a staff desperately anxious to give their best support to their sea-going brothers whom they so envied. One would be passed from desk to desk for the extraction of any new lessons learnt or tactical devices tried out and one left with the happy feeling, sometimes sadly lacking at HQ, that the shore staff knew they only existed to serve the sea-goers instead of vice versa.

One of the adjuncts of Derby House was a tactical school where, under the tireless command of Captain Roberts, sea experience was absorbed, digested and transformed into practical lessons on the tactical table. Here control teams from escort groups would come and would play tactical 'games' on the table in which every form of enemy attack known would be inflicted on them by a team of Wrens. These girls became so experienced in the tactics of convoy battle that they were able to save many a salt-encrusted sea-dog from making the errors which would inevitably lead to disaster to their convoys of model ships. Captain Roberts was a sufferer from consumption, never well and constantly in pain; but this never affected the enthusiasm and energy he brought to his rather thankless task.

Liverpool itself did not offer much in the way of relaxation, particularly after the blitz which devastated it to a great extent in 1941. I was fortunate, therefore, in usually being able to get away for a few days between convoys to join my wife and small son who had taken a house at Felpham near Bognor in Sussex. It was great fun unloading the things I had been able to bring back from across the Atlantic.

I remember, too, that before I was allowed to change out of my uniform into the anonymity of plain clothes, there was always a duty round of the food shops and the shopkeepers knew that this was the signal for something to come out from under the counter. To give them their due, it must be admitted that they accepted it with a good grace.

Back in Liverpool, the last few days before sailing again were given over to intensive training. Staff officers and captains of ships spent much of them at Captain Roberts' tactical school where they fought sanguinary imaginary battles on the tactical table.

Depth-charge parties were drilled until they could fire full patterns of depth-charges at fifteen-second intervals; asdic teams sank countless submarines on the synthetic attack teacher and communication staffs were exercised. Some of the training had its lighter moments. A very glamorous Wren officer initiated my younger officers into the mysteries of a new ciphering machine which was being introduced. These sessions took place in a pleasantly secluded hut at Gladstone Dock and it was remarkable what slow progress seemed to be made, requiring a great many lessons before the intricacies of the machine were mastered. Indeed the ubiquity of Wrens in every capacity ashore at Liverpool helped to make even the sterner occupations of our time in harbour occasions for hilarity and light relief. There was even a team of hard-swearing female ordnance ratings whose language when their hammers landed on a thumb instead of a breech lever used to make my gunner's mate blush.

Before sailing, my officers and I usually tried to arrange a dinner together at the Adelphi, miraculously surviving the devastation all round it. As the war progressed and Liverpool became filled with more and more servicemen, British and American, this became difficult to achieve.

But in *Hesperus* we were in a strong position, for in my office on board was a Writer rating, Val Thompson, who in private life was a prominent Liverpudlian, owning a chain of grocer's shops. To make sure of a table at the Adelphi, therefore, he would be tactfully approached and asked to use his influence.

Fortunately I never had occasion to discipline Writer Thompson, who indeed was a model rating, or perhaps I might have found myself *persona non grata* when I next tried to dine at the Adelphi!

We tended to become very parochial in our loyalties. Londonderry, for instance, being somewhat isolated from the remainder, became rather a law unto itself and was inclined to patronise those of us who lived, when in harbour, in the shadow of Derby House. Again, for a stranger such as we Liverpudlians to be diverted to Greenock for any reason was a horrible experience.

The great anchorage at the mouth of the Clyde was always choc-a-bloc with hundreds of ships, ranging from coasters to the huge passenger liners running as troopships. To the uninitiated they were berthed in the most complete confusion and with barely room to swing with the tide. The oiler to which one was invariably ordered on arrival was berthed in a remote and awkward spot.

Somehow one always arrived after dark and it was always raining cats and dogs and usually blowing a gale as well. In peacetime I have known the Firth of Clyde as one of the loveliest spots on earth with the sun shining on the purple hills, but those days seemed to vanish with the onset of war. Rain, wind, a complete ignorance of the berthing arrangements and a strict black-out, of course, all added up to a navigator's nightmare.

Cursing miserably, peering desperately through the downpour and the dark, one would creep tortuously through the seemingly solid mass of darkened ships. What we did not know until we had been in and out several times was that a lane down the side of the anchorage was in fact kept clear of ships, but somehow this vital piece of information was kept a deadly secret from 'foreigners' like us.

Similarly, the dragon that guarded the boom defences always knew when 'foreigners' were passing through his domain. He usually discovered that we were breaking some obscure rule of conduct and never failed to inform us in acidulated signals. Arrived at our anchorage finally at the Tail of the Bank, the odds were that there would be no peace, for the poor holding ground meant anchor watch and steam on the engines at the slightest blow. No—I preferred my own stamping ground at Liverpool with the lock gates safely slammed behind us and a berth alongside the jetty where nothing but a hurricane could disturb us.

Belfast, which became my base later in the war, was a newcomer to the scene, though trawlers had been based there before the new support groups were formed in 1944. An excellent team formed the base staff under Captain Borrett. The engineer officer, Commander Fenn Clark, his fiery spirit chafing at shore duty, worked like a black to see that the sea-goers should never sail with machinery anything but perfect.

The oriflamme of his flaming red beard would always be seen amongst the crowd on the jetty as we made fast and, with the first gangplank to go out, he would be on board for our lists of defects and getting his team to work.

The electrical team which maintained our asdics and radar were headed by Peter Frith and Roger Hawkey—the latter now Sir Roger, a baronet who manufactures water-closets, a combination so very typical of this age of social equality and streamlined plumbing!

CHAPTER 11

Defeat of a Wolf Pack

ON the 5th May the time came for B2 Group to leave Argentia again to rendezvous with the slow homeward-bound convoy, SC 129. On the following day we were once again going through the familiar routine of taking over escort, checking the convoy list against the ships present and rounding up stragglers.

The Battle of the Atlantic was working up to its climax. We knew that an unprecedented number of U-boats had been ranging the ocean for the last two months and convoys had had to fight their way through the enemy lines. May was likely to be the critical month. If the enemy onslaught could be held, the offensive should soon pass into our hands. For escorts were coming forward in increasing numbers, the immense output of American shipyards supplementing our own. In the air, the RAF were at long last allocating enough long-range aircraft to Coastal Command to enable them to close the gap of air cover in mid-Atlantic, and the new escort carriers would soon be at sea in sufficient numbers to accompany every convoy.

We were therefore on tip-toe in anticipation of the encounter that we knew must come. There was no longer any possibility of evading the U-boats—they were too thick for that.

However, for the first few days the convoy sailed on unmolested. I felt sure that 'B-Bar' in his H/F D/F cabinet would give us ample warning of our approach to any U-boat patrol lines. It was not until the afternoon of the 11th May that this first warning came. U-boats were about, but not so far in touch with our convoy, he estimated. I had learnt to trust implicitly in 'B-Bar's' estimates and up to date he had never been wrong. On this occasion, however, his guess as to the wave-length to watch must have been wrong. He had missed the vital first sighting signal. For, although a sweep to the horizon by *Whitehall* and *Clematis* produced nothing, at 1800 two ships in the convoy, *Antigone* and *Grado* were torpedoed in broad daylight and quickly sank. While I rapidly set in motion the search plan especially designed to take care of an emergency such as this, the rescue ship, *Melrose Abbey*, picked up the survivors and it was some slight comfort to know that only two men from one of the ships were missing.

These rescue ships, which at this stage of the Battle of the Atlantic were regular components of each convoy, were small steamers especially equipped for rescuing survivors from torpedoed ships. They performed a wonderful task at very great hazard, for by nature of their job they were forced to lie stopped, sitting targets, for long periods at the very time when U-boats were known to be near. I know full well what a naked, frightening feeling one has under such circumstances and I was always full of admiration for the unassuming courage of their crews.

Apart from rescuing a great many seamen who might not otherwise have survived, these ships freed the escort group commanders from the agonised decision they sometimes had to make, whether to ignore the call of humanity in order to keep the escorts to their primary task of preventing further sinkings by carrying the attack to the enemy—a grim decision that I am glad to say I never had to take though my standing orders for my group made it clear that survivors had to be ignored while an attack was in progress.

But I was now in a fury. Not only had a U-boat penetrated our defences in broad daylight but, for the first time in the nine months I had been with B2 Group, ships from a convoy escorted by us had been sunk. We were all very proud of our record which had thus been marred, and vengeance was called for. A thorough search for the culprit proved unsuccessful and it was with rage in my heart that I awaited the attack that I knew must come with nightfall.

For by now the bell from the H/F D/F office was ringing every few minutes and another report of a U-boat signalling close at hand would come through. But they were mostly from bearings astern or on the quarters of the convoy and I decided to hold my forces in until they could make their sorties without getting too far behind and so leaving the convoy short of escorts.

In *Hesperus* I had taken up a station for the night directly astern of the convoy. It seemed that the first attack must come from that direction unless it was postponed to the next day, by which time the U-boats would have been able to mass ahead of us. As darkness fell, I joined George Carlow on the bridge, where he was keeping the first watch (8–12) and as he conned the ship to and fro across the rear of the convoy we discussed the possibilities of the coming night. 'This is the likely quarter for an attack tonight, George,' I said. 'Warn the radar operators to keep a specially keen watch astern.' But George was fully alive to the situation and had already briefed them carefully.

A tense feeling of anticipation pervaded the whole ship's company. The look-outs relieved each other with brief, whispered words instead of their usual cheerful witticisms. Out there in the blackness we all knew a sinister menace lurked, and was slinking closer and closer to get in an attack. Our only doubt was the direction from which it would approach.

Presently Bill Ridley and Lyulph Stanley joined me in the chart room, unable to wait quietly down aft for the alarm they knew must come soon. 'Have all the "key" ratings been warned that "Action Stations" are almost certain during the night?' I asked Bill. 'We don't want to rout out the whole ship's company until the balloon goes up. They get little enough rest as it is.' 'Yes, all organised,' was Bill's reply. Coster, the senior asdic rating, was standing by to take over operation of the set at the first alarm. Down on the quarterdeck Mr Pritchard, the gunner, was prowling, checking and rechecking with his torpedo's gunner's mate that his depth-charge equipment was ready. In the shelter above the engine room hatch, 'Chiefy' Anderson and his chief ERA lurked, ready to take charge down below at the clang of the alarm bells. No-one could sleep that night.

Up on the bridge, the customary mugs of comforting, steaming cocoa had gone the rounds and the First Watch was nearly over when the report we had been waiting for came through from the radar office. 'Very small contact just come up, sir. Bearing 230 degrees. Range 5 miles.'

'This is it,' we cried with one voice. Leaving Lyulph to set his plotting table team to work, Bill and I tumbled out on to the compass platform. As the alarm gongs sounded their urgent call through the ship I swung *Hesperus* round to head for the bearing of the contact and rang down for full speed. Eyes strained through the darkness to get the first glimpse of the enemy. Suddenly, through the lenses of Otto Kretschmer's binoculars I could see the line of white which was the U-boat's wake. I altered course a few degrees to port to cut him off, hoping we might catch him before he could dive deep.

Racing along, we saw the white plumes of spray as he opened his vents and flooded his tanks to dive. As we passed over, the phosphorescent swirl left as he dived could be clearly seen.

'Get a first pattern away by eye,' I shouted to Bill. 'Shallow settings.' 'Fire one! Fire two! Fire three!' came the familiar cry in Bill's voice over the action 'inter-com'. He had needed no urging and the pattern went away perfectly timed.

As the depth-charges exploded, the tall columns of gleaming phosphorescent water soared up to stand momentarily like pillars of light before tumbling back into the sea in a torrent of foam.

I knew we could not have missed him by much and that he must be severely shaken at least. Now was the time to hammer him, to keep at him so as to give him no respite to repair damage. Reducing to a more moderate speed to give the asdics a chance we quickly picked up contact. As we expected, he had gone deep, so this was not a suitable target for the Hedgehog. Putting deep settings on the depth-charges, we ran in and gave him another full pattern. Once more we ran in and this time for good measure we added a one-ton depth-charge.

In the U-boat, *U 223*, the commander, Lieutenant Gerlach, saw with horror the shape of a destroyer emerging from a rain squall and bearing down on him. The curling bow waves of high speed left no doubt that the submarine had been sighted and that the destroyer was steering to ram.

With a yell, 'Take her down fast. Full speed ahead,' Gerlach and the look-outs dived for the conning-tower hatch. As the hatch slammed behind them, the U-boat was already heading desperately for the depths, where their only hope of safety lay. But the waters had hardly closed over it when the first pattern of depth-charges erupted all around. The boat was instantly plunged into darkness. The crew were hurled to the deck as the submarine was tossed and shaken by the appalling concussions. Out of control, it plunged on, deeper and deeper.

But as the drill so long and patiently practised against just such a crisis came into play, emergency lighting came on to give a fitful glow through the boat, control ratings staggered back to their stations and at 600 feet the dive was halted. Dead slow and utterly silent they must run now if they were to escape. Through the uncanny silence could be heard the 'pings' from the destroyer, and the steady volume of the note showed that she was in firm contact. Then came the beat of her propellers as she ran in for the attack, rising in a rapid crescendo till it became a roar as she passed overhead. As the depth-charges sank down, down to the U-boat's depth, the crew waited, tensed and agonised, for what seemed an eternity. Then the smashing, catastrophic explosions again, the U-boat rocked and hammered, the pressure hull cracking and creaking under the deadly thrusts. Even the robust emergency lighting failed now and through the blackness came the report that water was flooding into the fore compartments and the acrid smell of an electrical fire from the engine-room. With one main motor on fire and hardly an instrument or machine still functioning, the crew fought to halt the downward plunge which had again developed and had already reached 700 feet. As they did so, with the roar of an express train their tormentor passed overhead again and another series of concussions threw everything into utter confusion. Another such attack and it must be the end. Gerlach realised that there was nothing for it but to blow tanks and try to fight it out, or escape, on the surface.

Aft, on *Hesperus'* quarter-deck, the depth-charge parties struggled like demons after each attack to reload the throwers and chutes for the next one. Fifteen seconds they had achieved at the driller back in Gladstone Dock, but, though the driller had a tilting deck which simulated to some extent the motion of a ship at sea, the real thing was infinitely more disconcerting. As the ship lurched and rolled, the 750-lb. canisters seemed to take savage and vindictive life. Swinging on their tackles as they were hoisted up into the throwers they could crush and mangle an unwary handler. With the ship under helm, seas came curling over the side and the struggling men were up to their waists in icy, swirling water.

I do not guarantee that they beat their fifteen-second record, but under the leadership of Mr Pritchard, the gunner, they never failed to have a full pattern ready when called for. At the same time the ready-use stowages were kept 'topped-up' by further charges hoisted up from the magazine and manhandled along the deck. Amongst the depth-charge party there was rarely a break for a breather or to wonder how the action was going.

As *Hesperus* steered to attack again, the asdic operators reported the noise of blowing tanks and then, close ahead of us we saw the U-boat surface and lie, stopped. He was too close for the 4.7-inch guns to be brought to bear, but the Oerlikon 20-mm guns sprang into action and some of the U-boat's crew, who were making as if to man their gun, were swept into the sea by this fire. The U-boat passed close down our side and as it came abreast of our stern, depth-charges set to explode at the minimum depth of 50 feet were fired. Again I turned the ship and ran in to repeat the performance. But this was a tough nut to crack, for, to my astonishment the U-boat managed to get its engines turning and got under way. With our signal searchlights illuminating it, the 4.7-inch guns opened fire and scored several hits.

Though in desperate straits, the Germans were by no means ready to throw in the sponge. The hail of shells killed and wounded several of them, and drove the remainder from the bridge to take shelter in the conning-tower. But down below the crew remained at their action stations and, as Gerlach saw *Hesperus* bearing down on him to loose further depth-charges he gave the order to fire a torpedo from the stern tube. But with only the narrow end-on view to aim at, the torpedo sped harmlessly by. He fired four more shots but with *Hesperus* keeping her bow or stern pointed at the U-boat, she was an almost impossible target. In desperation, Gerlach tried to ram his pursuer but his boat was no longer in a condition to manœuvre.

The U-boat came again to a standstill, yet there was no sign of it sinking. It just lay there at bay, sinister and dangerous yet. 'What in God's name do I do now?' I thought to myself. 'I must keep under way and heading for her or we will be a sitting target for a torpedo.' How right I was, too, for unknown to us, the U-boat was indeed fighting back, but we were too difficult a target end-on.

Meanwhile the only gun in *Hesperus* that could be brought to bear continued to shoot by the light of our searchlights and scored several hits. But, as we ran slowly in towards the U-boat, the gun could no longer be depressed sufficiently.

For a moment I considered ramming the submarine and so finishing her off quickly, but then I recalled the state of *Hesperus* after the last occasion of ramming—her keel twisted back, fore compartments flooded and, above all, the asdic dome wiped off and the asdic out of action. With the convoy still under attack and a long way to go, I could not afford that. Besides we had been officially discouraged from ramming since the tragic loss of 'Harry' Tait and *Harvester*.

'Bill,' I said to Ridley, standing beside me on the compass

platform, 'do you think we could roll her over by a gentle ram so as not to damage the ship?' 'Try it, sir,' was his reply. 'We are getting very short of depth-charges and we are going to need plenty before we are finished with this convoy. I don't want to have to use any more to finish off this bastard.'

So try it I did. With a gentle bump I laid *Hesperus'* bow against the U-boat's side and kept the engines going slowly ahead. The submarine rolled over on to its beam ends, lay like that for a moment, but then as our bow slid down its length, sluggishly righted itself. But it was obviously lying much lower in the water and I felt its end must be near. Yet as we ran out again to give the guns another chance, a torpedo raced by, leaving a phosphorescent trail and narrowly missing us. This was indeed a dauntless and dangerous enemy!

But even as we turned to go into the attack again, the U-boat's crew could be seen on deck and one or two were seen to jump overboard. 'He's finished,' I thought, 'and none too soon. The convoy must be thirty miles or more ahead and I must get back to it at once.'

Precious time could not be spared to stay and deliver the *coup de grâce* and pick up the survivors, with all the delay that would entail. Laying the ship on a course to rejoin the convoy I left the sinking U-boat to its fate.

On the bridge of *U 223*, Lieutenant Gerlach, realising that he could fight no more and believing that his ship must soon sink, had ordered his crew on deck but not yet to abandon ship. One wounded man fell overboard and was lost. Another, mistaking the order, jumped into the water. Fire from the destroyer then ceased and to Gerlach's astonishment, she steamed off and was quickly lost to sight in the darkness. Gradually it was borne in on the German's mind that at the eleventh hour he had been reprieved. The crew were ordered back to their stations and set to work feverishly to try to make their U-boat seaworthy. With the bilges full of broken glass and débris, pumping was a difficult and laborious task. For twelve hours they laboured like madmen and by four o'clock the next afternoon they were under way and limping for St Nazaire which they reached twelve days later. It was a remarkable piece of engineering and seamanship on their part and if their story were not well authenticated it might be hard to believe.

But even more astonishing is the story of the seaman who jumped overboard. He quickly vanished from sight of the crew of *U 223* and for several hours he floated in his lifejacket in the rough sea. He had long given up hope of rescue, when, to his utter amazement, another submarine, *U 359*, surfaced some fifty yards from him. He managed to attract their attention, was picked up and eventually rejoined his incredulous shipmates.

Hurrying after the convoy, I had time to pick up the threads of the situation. A study of the H/F D/F reports showed that a dozen or more U-boats were chasing the convoy, trying evidently to get to a position ahead in which they could lie in waiting. I knew that they would not attack in daylight until they had achieved such a position and by now the dawn was approaching and would give us a brief respite.

As the morning wore on we watched the bearings of enemy transmissions from those conveniently chattering U-boats, drawing steadily ahead. *Whitehall* was sent out after one on the starboard bow but without result. And then at 11.30 a signal was heard from close ahead. This was what I had been waiting for and I quickly turned *Hesperus* to the bearing and raced off at high speed. 'Not more than ten miles away,' had been 'B-Bar's' estimate, so at nine miles I reduced speed for the asdic to come into action and almost immediately came the cry 'Contact' from the asdic control room.

Before there was time to classify the echo coming back to us, and as I scanned the sea ahead, I was astonished to see the tip of a periscope moving across our course. With a frenzied shout to order shallow settings on a pattern of depth-charges, I set *Hesperus* at full speed to intercept the U-boat. The periscope dipped as we dashed forward but I was able to gauge by eye the right moment to fire and as the depth-charges went off I felt sure that the U-boat must be at least heavily damaged.

Turning to complete the job, contact was gained on the asdic and a steady attack delivered on the target which was already very deep. Noises of escaping air and other signs of the submarine being in desperate straits came to the ears of Petty Officer Coster on the asdic. One more attack we made to make sure of the job and, as we searched to regain contact, we felt through our hull the underwater explosion which usually accompanies the crushing of the pressure hull of a submarine at great depth.

I circled the spot for a while and then running over it was grimly gratified to see a spreading pool of oil with floating débris and smashed woodwork obviously from the interior of the U-boat. Quickly picking up a few specimens in evidence, on one of which was found a gruesome piece of flesh, we returned to our station with the convoy. So ended *U 186*.

Meanwhile, from the remainder of the group, signals were coming in which showed that the convoy was more or less surrounded by U-boats which were being sighted at frequent intervals as they steamed at high speed to get ahead. At 1500 *Whitehall* and *Heather*, searching down the bearing of an enemy transmission, sighted two, forced them to dive and made attacks on them but were unable to hold contact and had to return to their station empty-handed. An hour later *Sweetbriar* sighted one, and on giving chase came in sight of yet another. Unfortunately the U-boats when surfaced could outrun the Flower Class corvettes and after a brief stern-chase *Sweetbriar* had to give up and return to her station. While this was going on *Clematis* on the other side of the convoy also sighted two U-boats and vainly gave chase.

It was maddening to be so close to so many enemies and be able to do nothing about it. For in *Hesperus* we were by now so low in depth-charges that we could not afford to use any unless a U-boat was in a position of real menace. Replacements were available in our tanker with the convoy, but the heavy Atlantic swell was causing us all to roll so heavily that it was not possible to risk trying to go alongside her to transfer them.

By the evening, however, we knew that the U-boats had worked ahead of the convoy's track and unless we could do something to keep them down to let the convoy draw ahead, a mass attack that night would be inevitable. At 1830 *Whitehall* was sent out to scout on the starboard bow while *Hesperus* searched to port. In a short time a signal came in from Bell in *Whitehall* that he had no less than three U-boats in sight on the surface. I quickly took *Hesperus* off in support, the only other ship in the escort with the speed to close the U-boats and force them to dive. Very soon *Whitehall's* U-boats came in sight on the horizon and we set off in chase.

I suppose it would not have been unnatural if by this time and with such a concentration of U-boats threatening our convoy, we had begun to feel dismayed at the task facing us. Instead, however, I remember the feeling of exhilaration which permeated the whole ship. We felt we were more than a match for the team opposing us. Lyulph Stanley, always our licensed buffoon, set the tone when, on hearing the look-out report a third U-boat in sight, exclaimed piteously, 'We are beset! Oh me poor wife and children!'

As we streaked along to join *Whitehall*, I tried to formulate a plan to deal with the situation. These German submarines could make 17 knots surfaced so that to overtake them, if they remained on the surface, would be a long business. Both *Hesperus* and *Whitehall* had only rudimentary gunnery control equipment as much of it had been removed in favour of radar, radio and anti-submarine equipment, but, with their solitary fore 4.7-inch guns, fire was opened at maximum range. There was little or no hope of scoring a hit on these tiny targets. The gunlayers at first could not, indeed, even see their target and the guns were brought on to the right bearing by swinging the ship. With only single shots it was very difficult to see whether we were going over or short and, in fact, the U-boats were really in no danger at all. Fortunately they did not realise this and, as we slowly drew nearer and fire became a trifle less inaccurate, they dived one after the other.

This, of course, virtually immobilised the U-boats, for their submerged speed was low and, with destroyers hunting them, they would keep their speed down to a minimum to avoid being detected by their propeller noises. Furthermore they were now blind and the convoy might be able to escape if they could be kept down.

There was just time before dark, which made such manœuvres with a mass of shipping difficult, to order a drastic alteration of course of the convoy which would not only leave the U-boats uncertain of which direction the convoy had taken, but would put them once again in the position of having a long chase if they wished to get close enough to attack.

While this was being done *Hesperus* and *Whitehall* searched through the estimated diving position of the nearest U-boat in the hope of getting in a depth-charge attack before the time came to get back to the convoy for the night, when every escort would be needed there. Contact was obtained and both *Whitehall* and *Hesperus* made attacks but asdic conditions were not good and I did not feel that we had inflicted much damage.

The pressure of time was heavy on me, too. There were probably nine other U-boats shaping course to attack the convoy as soon as it was dark and we could not linger to hunt these three systematically. Nights are short at that season too, and it was unlikely that these would have time to overtake and attack before dawn. So I called off the attack.

Back at the convoy I took *Hesperus* again to my favourite station, right astern of the convoy. Not only did I feel that that was the most likely direction of attack but I was able to keep the whole area occupied by the convoy and screen ahead of me and could at once see if any activity occurred. Everyone in the escorts was keyed up to the highest pitch.

In *Hesperus* our unshaven faces were beginning to take on a haggard look. We had been more or less continuously in action for thirty-six hours and there had been no sleep for anyone the previous night. We looked a piratical lot but it was exhilarating to see with what zest all hands were looking forward to another brush with the enemy in the night that lay before us.

It seemed certain that a heavy attack must be brewing up. I was astonished, therefore, when hour followed quiet hour while the convoy crept on unmolested.

This calm was broken suddenly by a radio call from *Whitehall*. Bell had a contact on his radar screen and was off to investigate. On my radar screen I watched the blob of light that was *Whitehall* move off from his position on the screen, while my well-trained team adjusted their positions, unbidden, to cover the gap thus left. 'Contact lost' was Bell's next report, presumably as the U-boat dived. 'Carrying out asdic search', he reported. Even as I was giving the order which would send *Clematis* to support *Whitehall*, a signal came in from *Heather* on the other side of the convoy to say that he, too, had a radar contact and I had to think again. For if this was a concerted attack beginning I could not afford to have too many of the meagre escort away from the screen. I cancelled the order and both *Whitehall* and *Heather* were left to fend for themselves.

Time dragged by as I waited for further news from them, but neither managed to make definite contact and as soon as the convoy had passed the danger zone they were recalled.

As peace and quiet settled down again, the feeling of expectancy began to seep away. In spite of repeated doses of Pusser's thick cocoa and the keen air that swept our faces on the bridge, sleep began to pluck at our eyelids and we began to notice how tired we all were.

Abruptly we were galvanised into action once again by a report from our own radar operator. As on the previous night a contact had appeared astern of the convoy. The situation was identical and action followed on similar lines. As we turned to attack, the U-boat dived and almost at once the asdic team was in contact.

Our first attack sent the U-boat deep at once and here we found ourselves in a maddening situation, for the few depth-charges we had remaining were of the light type and could not be detonated down to the depths at which hunted U-boats could go. For when the capabilities of deep diving of the German submarines had been realised in 1942 a modified heavy depth-charge had been devised which could be set to sink to 800 feet before exploding. Now, after the many encounters which we had had since leaving harbour, not only was *Hesperus* down to her last fourteen charges but she had no 'heavies' left at all.

So long as the U-boat stayed deep, it was immune to our attacks. The only solution was to call back a corvette from the escort to help us out, though I was loath to denude the screen while attacks by other U-boats were expected at any moment. While we patrolled back and forth over the U-boat, *Clematis* was ordered to join *Hesperus*. The next three-quarters of an hour were a strange interlude for, although I was unable to attack the U-boat, I steered *Hesperus* again and again over it as though I was attacking.

Down in the U-boat, as it crept along at 700 feet, at its slowest and most silent speed, the suspense must have been appalling. The crew could have been under no illusion that their attacker had lost touch for the sound of the 'ping' trained steadily on them would be heard in their hydro-phones as well as the beat of the propellers driving *Hesperus* through the water over their heads, rising to a roar as we passed over, then fading as the agonised crew waited for the bursting of the depth-charges that must surely be on their way down. As they breathed sighs of relief at their respite, the same menacing sound would start again. 'This time the charges must surely come!' they must have thought.

If we had been free agents, we could have hung on and held the U-boat down till he was forced to come up, gasping for air or with his batteries exhausted. But with the convoy beset, we could not stay away from it so long.

At last *Clematis* bustled up at her maximum speed of 15 knots and, passing bearings and ranges to her, she was guided to the position of the U-boat. Quickly she gained firm contact and I felt confident I could leave her to finish the job we had started. As we sped after our convoy the thudding of *Clematis's* charges could be felt through our hull.

But how I wish now that I could have stayed and helped *Clematis* to keep contact, for after a couple of attacks she lost touch and never regained it and could find no evidence that the U-boat had been sunk.

The expected attack on the convoy developed no further and I could well have kept *Hesperus* back to see the end of the job. But it was not a risk I could take. Satisfactory as it was to kill U-boats, those fateful instructions that the 'safe and timely arrival of the convoy' was our main objective were always in the forefront of my mind.

The rest of the night passed quickly and daylight found our slow convoy serenely plodding along. It was something of an anti-climax, after all the dashing to and fro of the preceding day and the constant sightings of the wolf-pack waiting to close.

But, as with real wolf-packs, it seemed as though a bold front and an occasional kill was enough to keep them at a distance. What a difference from the early days of the Battle of the Atlantic when a handful of U-boats played havoc with our convoys! Radar and H/F D/F had transformed the situation around the convoys and the constant fear of being surprised on the surface by patrolling and escorting aircraft was steadily wearing down the morale of the U-boat crews. For the first time a so-called wolf-pack with their prey in sight had most of them slunk off without making an attempt to get to grips.

Later, when the figures for U-boat sinkings for May were known—no less than 45—and these signs of lost morale were placed alongside them, it began to be said with quiet confidence that the Battle of the Atlantic had been won. And, indeed, it had. Though a large number of U-boats continued at sea for the rest of the war, never again was the vital trans-atlantic supply-line seriously threatened.

With the threat to the convoy SC 129 disposed of, all our other problems sorted themselves out. The Atlantic smoothed itself and *Hesperus* was able—too late alas!—to replenish her stock of depth-charges. *Whitehall*, whose movements had had to be restricted owing to shortage of fuel, was able to top up with oil.

What finally sent me to my bunk for some overdue sleep was the arrival in the vicinity of our old friend *Biter*. With her Swordfish patrolling round the horizon I could rest with a quiet mind. The only drawback to the great improvement in the weather was that visibility became extreme so that U-boats could not be surprised from the air and were able to get safely below the surface before an aircraft could pounce on them. Otherwise the defeated wolf-pack which was still snapping half-heartedly round our heels might have suffered further losses.

By the 16th May the convoy was safely through the danger area. The loss of the two ships still rankled but we felt we had avenged them.

CHAPTER 12

Hunter-Killer

DURING the winter of 1943–44 and the following spring, the convoy escorts had frequently been augmented on their homeward journeys by a new type of ship, coming to the Royal Navy from American building yards in a steady stream. These were designated by the Americans 'British Destroyer-Escorts' and known to us as 'Captain' Class frigates, all being named after naval captains of the days of the French Wars. They were built at incredible speed using the new technique of welding together prefabricated sections. The fastest time achieved was fifty-four days from laying the keel to completion, which was an astounding feat when one remembers the complex electrical and electronic gear fitted, with its great lengths of complicated wiring, apart from the normal construction of the hull and the fitting of the machinery.

One of the principal bottlenecks in the mass production of warships driven by steam turbines is the production of the massive gear-wheels which are necessary to transmit the power of the fast-revolving turbines to the relatively slow propellers which at 20 knots would probably be turning at some 200 revs a minute. To overcome this, and as very high speeds were not essential, the designers discarded the normal geared turbines and substituted electric drive. There were two types of these frigates, steam-turbine-electric and diesel-electric. The former had a top speed of 24 knots, the latter of 18 knots.

The ships appeared to be a compromise between American and British design. The bridge was of the open type at that time favoured by the Royal Navy, and the asdics and depth-charge equipment were also British. The machinery and electrical gear were American and the hull was on finer lines than we go in for—more 'herring-gutted' as we call it. The result of this last characteristic was to give them a really fierce roll in a seaway. In order to make them a little less lively, on arrival in the UK they were fitted with stowages for a huge number of depth-charges on the upper deck. This made for a slower roll though even then it took only three seconds to complete a roll from over on one side to over on the other. They were very tiring ships to live in in a seaway and exasperating, as nothing could be left unsecured and even such normally stable things as the rubber erasers for the chart table would perpetually leap to the deck and hide themselves just when urgently wanted.

The principal weakness of these ships was the main gunnery armament. I cannot imagine where the Americans found the short-barrelled 3-inch blunderbusses with which they were furnished—elephant guns, I remember, we nicknamed them. They fired a minute shell of, I suspect, solid steel with no explosive charge for on the only occasion we fired them in anger they were seen to bounce off the target without exploding. I had no confidence whatever in these weapons. The DEs which the Americans commissioned for their own navy had 5-inch guns, a very different class of weapon.

But gunnery was a secondary requirement in the Atlantic and the good points of these little ships far outweighed the bad. And with the great strengthening of our escort forces which their addition represented, it was possible to form an additional number of support groups to carry the offensive against the U-boats a stage further.

It was with mixed feelings that I received orders, on arrival in Liverpool in March, 1944, to leave my faithful *Hesperus* and take command of one of these frigates, the *Bickerton*, and form what was to be known as the 5th Escort Group. With the withdrawal from the North Atlantic of most of the U-boats after their defeat in the spring of 1943, convoy escort through the following winter had certainly been a monotonous and unexciting duty and the idea of being given a more or less roving command was very attractive. But I had hoped that I might be able to take *Hesperus* and lead a group of destroyers. I had spent altogether three years of the war in *Hesperus*, had commanded her through the Norwegian campaign and in many an exciting and successful convoy action.

She had carried me through three Atlantic winters and never faltered and those turbines, whose first trials from Thorneycroft's yard I had witnessed in January, 1940, still ran with the silkiness of a sewing-machine. I knew every rivet and plate in her and I wanted no other ship under me.

The thought of leaving her was heartbreaking. Though I was to be allowed to take with me my staff officers, Bill Ridley (who at great self-sacrifice chose to come with me instead of getting a command of his own) and Lyulph Stanley, the remainder of our happy company had to be left behind.

Fortunately there was no time for regrets. The two ships were alongside one another and I hurriedly turned over *Hesperus* to my relief, Commander Legassick RNR, stepped aboard *Bickerton*, and sailed immediately for Belfast where my new group was to form.

The 5th Escort Group consisted of six frigates, three of which, *Bickerton*, *Aylmer* and *Bligh*, were turbo-electric 24-knotters and the others, *Kempthorne*, *Keats* and *Goodson*, diesel-electric 18-knotters. The COs were all new to me except for little Jackie Cooper, ex-*Sweetbriar*, who came, monocle and enthusiasm complete, to command *Bligh*. Unlike my first trip in *Walker*, I was allowed a period to 'work-up' my group and, being all new ships, with COs accustomed to the sturdy little Flower-class corvettes and not used to the lively destroyer-like DEs, such a shake-down was badly needed. As soon as possible the group sailed for exercises in the Irish Sea, off Larne, and while learning the idiosyncrasies of my own ship I started to put them through their paces. How I missed my faithful B2 Group and their well-drilled teamwork and how I missed my wonderful Chief Yeoman of Signals Wilkinson and his staff of signalmen. My temper was short and my signals often sulphuric.

I fear that a reputation for giving short shrift to incompetents had come with me to my new group. Perhaps the fact that one of the ships was named after the famous Captain

Bligh of the *Bounty*, who incidentally was not the monster portrayed in the well-known film but an efficient officer and a sound seaman who rose to flag rank, may have predisposed my COs to fear the worst. Fortunately Bill and Lyulph were able to reassure them and very quickly we became a team and ready for the fray. On 21st April, 1944, we sailed for our first operation.

Our orders were to act in support of the escort of Convoy ONS 233. This promised to be a very quiet assignment, for the Atlantic convoys were by now shuttling across the Atlantic almost entirely unmolested, the U-boats working further afield in the hopes of finding easier targets.

It would, however, serve as a shake-down cruise for our still inexperienced team and the usual Atlantic gales which beset us for the first three days certainly taught us the capabilities of our ships. A large proportion of the ships' companies had hardly been to sea before, except to bring their ships back from building in the States, where they had lived on the fat of the land and had grown soft.

The first days were therefore more of a 'throw-up' than a 'shake-down' for them. The wicked rolling had in most cases worked a cure by the time the weather moderated on the 25th.

On this day we were withdrawn from support of the convoy, which was under no threat, and were sent off to search an area where a U-boat had been reported. It was alarming to find ourselves being employed on the same wild-goose chase as in the early bad old days of 1940, but the fact was that in this period before the invasion of Normandy, the U-boats were so completely in eclipse in the Atlantic that there was little for our vastly expanded escort forces to do. It was all good practice for us and we were glad of the opportunity.

The following day, 26th April, fresh orders gave us hopes of livelier employment for we were instructed to join the escort carrier *Vindex* (Captain H. T. T. Bayliss RN) which was operating with the 9th Escort Group. I had great confidence that the combination of a carrier's aircraft and my group would bring us a dividend, providing any enemy were about. It was disappointing to find that apparently rather aimless sweeps were to be our task.

After three days of it we had just about had enough and the enthusiasm with which we had set out was rapidly seeping away when the picture was transformed by an assignment which really promised results.

It was the German practice to maintain in mid-Atlantic one or more U-boats for the sole purpose of transmitting, twice a day, a weather report. These reports, of course, were vital to their long-range forecasts of the weather in and around Europe. As they performed an entirely passive role and need not surface for more than the time required to charge batteries and send off their weather reports, they were normally in very little danger of detection.

A previous attempt to hunt down one of these U-boats by an escort group, acting without a carrier, had ended in failure, but a combination of aircraft patrols and H/F D/F obtaining bearings each time the U-boat transmitted her report offered great promise. It was with renewed enthusiasm therefore that we received orders to proceed to a position 52N and 30W with *Vindex* to see what we could do.

The 9th Escort Group left us at this time, so half my group, the slower diesel-engined division, took over the duty of screening the carrier while I continued to operate with the remainder, independently of, but in co-operation with, *Vindex* where Captain Bayliss as the senior officer present commanded the whole operation.

If we were to achieve success the utmost patience would be required. First we would have to get roughly in the area of the U-boat's position. This could be given us by the Admiralty from information obtained from the powerful D/F stations on shore.

Having got somewhere near the submarine, we must hope to pick up its transmissions on our own D/F sets, get a bearing and, by directing an aircraft quickly in the right direction, achieve a sighting which would pin-point our target. This was what we hoped to do and if I had still had my miracle man Harold Walker with me in the H/F D/F office, the U-boat would have soon been 'in the bag'. But like the rest of the crews, the H/F D/F operators were newly-trained and quite inexperienced, so the trap took a little longer to spring.

On the 2nd May we were nearing the position given us by the Admiralty and the morning weather report was duly intercepted and a bearing obtained. The U-boat was still some distance away so that we did not hope from this one bearing to do more than fine down the area to be searched and I confidently expected to get more information from the evening transmission. To my disgust when the time came not one of the H/F D/F teams in the group managed to intercept the signal, nor did they do any better for the next two days.

Without these signals our task was hopeless, for a U-boat free to manœuvre could always evade our searches. To give the devil his due, it was obvious that in the U-boat our possession of H/F D/F was known and respected. We knew from Admiralty information that the frequency on which the weather reports were being transmitted was never the same twice in succession and this made our task a little more difficult.

But at last in the early morning of 5th May, the D/F operators in *Bickerton* succeeded in detecting the U-boat's transmission and estimated that it was fairly close. Passing this longed-for information to *Vindex*, I took the 1st Division, *Bickerton*, *Aylmer* and *Bligh*, to sweep in the estimated direction of the U-boat. Though we failed to get contact the area to be searched had been further reduced and, in fact, we later learned that we passed within sight of the U-boat on this search. But, if aircraft could be flown that night, there was a good chance of their detecting the enemy. Luck was with us and the weather was reasonable, though incidentally *Vindex* had ideas of her own as to what was suitable weather for flying and used to keep her aircraft up in the most fearful conditions and with amazing success.

When night fell Captain Bayliss had planned his air patrols so that they could swamp the suspected area and, soon after midnight, success rewarded their efforts when Lieut. Huggins RNVR, flying a Swordfish, sighted the U-boat, forced it to dive and marked the position with a flare. The position was only twelve miles from the carrier but considerably further from my 1st Division which was searching further afield. Bayliss therefore detached *Keats* (Lieut.-Commander Keene RNR) from his screen to hunt, while joyfully I swung *Bickerton*, *Aylmer* and *Bligh* round to hurry back to join in.

Keats, arriving at the marker left by the aircraft, started to search, but the U-boat had had the best part of an hour to get clear and might have gone in any direction. Nevertheless, a carefully planned search brought success when, at four o'clock in the morning, *Keats*' radar operator reported a contact. Running down the bearing, Keene sighted nothing but soon picked up an asdic contact and set to to attack it.

Unfortunately it has to be recorded that the U-boat captain outwitted Keene on this occasion, perhaps by the successful use of an SBT. Like the rest of us, Keene had a 'green' asdic crew and, having made their first attack, it would seem as though they fastened either on to the SBT or on to the echo given off by the disturbed water where charges had burst and which is, of course, renewed at each attack.

They made good use of the lessons learnt for, later in the war, Keene and the *Keats* succeeded in sinking two other U-boats.

On this occasion, however, the U-boat slid off and the crew, laughing up their sleeves, listened to the distant banging of depth-charges and congratulated themselves on a wily piece of evasion. But they laughed too soon, for, lulled into a false sense of security, they did not hear the noise of propellers as the 1st Division drew near. We were still doing 20 knots, the highest speed at which our asdics would function at all efficiently, as we reached a position some three miles from *Keats*. At that point the asdic picked up a contact, clear and loud, out on the port bow. Quick action is necessary at that speed.

Firstly, the ship must be swung bows on to the contact so as to present the smallest possible target to a possible torpedo attack, for at this stage it is by no means certain who is the hunter and who the hunted, and torpedoes may already be racing through the water on a course to intercept the ship should she continue to steer straight ahead.

At the same time speed must be reduced, not only to give the asdic team time to get all their instruments lined up, to work out the course and speed of the submarine, and to pass the necessary information to the bridge for an accurate attack to be delivered, but also to reduce the propeller noises so as not to attract any acoustic torpedo that may have been fired.

Signals must be passed out to consorts to warn them that we are in contact and to get them to conform to our movements. All this takes less time to do than to say and very soon *Bickerton* was heading for the contact and nosing towards it at slow speed with her crew tense at Action Stations.

The asdic team was functioning smoothly and confidently and their reports came steadily from the loudspeaker on the bridge.

'Contact Firm—Classified Submarine.'

'Range 1,500 yards—Inclination opening.'

'Target moving left.'

Bill Ridley controlling, earphones on his head and a rapt look on his face as he concentrated on listening to the echoes, gave me a 'thumbs up' sign to indicate that we were definitely on the genuine article.

The range came steadily down and, on the plot, the submarine's position was marked as each echo came back. He was on a steady course, going very slowly and seemed unaware of our approach.

Then, with the range at 700 yards, the echoes faded and died. Bill quickly adjusted the asdic sweep to cover a larger arc in case the operators had made a mistake, but no contact resulted.

'He's way down deep, sir, I'm sure,' he said, and I felt certain he was right. Remembering the difficulty we had had in destroying other deep U-boats when in *Hesperus*, I at once decided to put into use the 'Creeping Attack' invented by Captain 'Johnnie' Walker. This had been devised because a deep U-boat, well handled, could evade a normal depth-charge attack. The propellers of the attacking ship could be heard approaching and by altering course at the right moment the U-boat could get a safe distance from the explosions. For in the attacking ship, contact with a deep submarine would be lost at a range of 700 or 800 yards and from that time onwards any alteration by the U-boat would be undetected. Furthermore, even the time taken by the charges to sink down to the depth of the submarine was long enough for the submarine to get out of their way.

The creeping attack made use of the fact that the U-boat's hydrophones were masked by its own propeller noises from hearing a ship coming up slowly from right astern. So one ship would hold contact at about 1,000 yards astern of the U-boat and would direct a consort up the U-boat's wake at the slowest possible speed to overtake. Then, as the consort crept into position over the unsuspecting U-boat, at an order from the directing ship, a stream of twenty-six depth-charges set to their maximum depth would go down to explode accurately around their target.

I had practised this manœuvre when working-up the group and now, opening the range to get into firm contact again, I called upon Jackie Cooper in the *Bligh* to play the part of attacking ship.

Going dead slow and conned by my orders over the radio-telephone, *Bligh* crept by us and up the wake of the U-boat. The suspense was terrific as *Bligh's* range, taken from the portable range-finder on my bridge, mounted slowly towards that of the submarine given by the asdic. Gripping the compass binnacle in an agony of anticipation, I listened to Lyulph Stanley reading off the ranges of *Bligh* and the asdic operators chanting that of the submarine. At last the two ranges coincided and I passed the order to Jackie Cooper, 'Stand By'.

I must get *Bligh* a little bit ahead of the target to allow for its movement ahead as the charges are sinking to their depth. Her range mounted with exasperating slowness, 10 yards, 20 yards beyond the U-boat and then at 50 yards the moment had come. My throat was so dry with excitement that I just managed to croak out the word 'Fire!' But the chief yeoman of signals passed it on the radio telephone loud and clear and I saw the first charge splash into the water from *Bligh's* stern. It had a long way to sink before exploding and it was not until half a dozen or more of the succession of twenty-six had been dropped that the first concussion thudded through the ship.

One after the other, we could see the charges splashing into the water from her stern and others arching through the air as the throwers were fired. Suddenly we saw one charge burst prematurely, very shallow. A shower of soot came up from *Bligh's* funnel and we could see her whipping with the shock of the explosion close under her stern as a tall column of water rose up to fall with a thunder onto her quarter-deck. But her depth-charge team was equal to the occasion and continued with precision to get the rest of the charges away.

A hundred fathoms deep, all was quiet in the U-boat and the crew had no inkling of the death that was sinking down through the water to them. With a shattering concussion the first charge went off alongside, plunging the boat in darkness. Another and another, creating utter confusion and cracking the stout pressure hull allowing the seas to pour in. 'To the surface at all costs' was the despairing thought of the U-boat's captain, Werner Wendt. A frenzied order sent the high-pressure air forcing its way into the ballast tanks and sending the U-boat with a rush to the surface, even as further charges exploded around it to wreak further damage.

On *Bickerton's* bridge, as the last charge thudded out, I saw a cascade of foam and spray as the U-boat shot to the surface amongst the brown scummy patches left by the explosions.

In the few moments it was in sight the twisted, buckled plating of the U-boat's conning tower could be seen, evidence that at least one depth-charge had found its mark. As I gave the order to take *Bickerton* in to deliver the *coup de grâce*, out of the sky with a roar dived a Swordfish from *Vindex*, flown by the Squadron Commander, Lieut.-Commander Sheffield RNVR, to drop two depth-charges neatly one each side of the U-boat. The columns of water subsided and the U-boat slid stern-first below the surface. As *Bickerton* arrived over the spot, the tell-tale explosions of her pressure hull collapsing in the depths were felt through the ship and I knew all was over. A few, very few figures were left swimming and these were picked up and made prisoner.

We were all, of course, enormously elated, but I was especially pleased for, once again, as in my first trip in *Walker*, the group had been 'blooded' on its first operation. From now onwards I knew we would be a team, co-ordinated, fully-trained and able to cock our chests in the ports of Western Approaches.

It was a wonderful piece of luck and I remember signalling to the group in my elation that from now onwards they could call themselves 'The Fighting Fifth'—a flamboyant gesture very much out of character for me, but I believe it was enjoyed. It was also, of course, a textbook operation of what later became known, by adoption from American phraseology, as a 'Hunter-Killer' group. To select a U-boat in the middle of the wide Atlantic and by co-ordination of H/F D/F, air search and asdic hunt, attack and wipe it off the map, had not been done before and *Vindex* and the 5th Escort Group were proud of themselves.

Presently from the survivors of the U-boat, *U 765*, among whom was its captain, Korvetten Kapitän Werner Wendt, we learnt their story. As we thought, they had successfully evaded *Keats*' initial attack, had suffered no damage and were peacefully and quietly effacing themselves when all hell broke loose as *Bligh's* 'plaster' erupted around them.

Amazingly they had not heard the 1st Division arriving, although we were doing 20 knots when we first gained contact, and so successful had our 'Creep' been that they had no forewarning of an impending attack. I always hoped that 'Johnnie' Walker heard how we put his tactic to good use, but I never found out as, except for an exchange of signals as our groups passed on opposite courses one day in the Channel, I did not meet him again before he died. It was a great satisfaction to me that when that greatest of U-boat killers was buried at sea, it was in my gallant *Hesperus* that he made his last journey down the Mersey and past the Bar Lightship.

Hesperus, with her record of five U-boats to her credit, was worthy of him.

At a time when things were quiet, I had Captain Wendt brought to my cabin. We had a drink together, and I tried to find out what sort of a fellow he was. He spoke good English and indeed claimed to have been employed before the war in England by the Westminster Bank.

I am afraid that my only feeling towards him was one of dislike. He was an arrogant, strutting little braggart. One of his boasts was that he had been First-Lieutenant in the U-boat commanded by Von Bulow and that he had seen the American aircraft carrier *Ranger* sink after being torpedoed. He stuck to his story for some time but was finally convinced that *Ranger* was very much alive and kicking. Thereupon he modified his tale by saying that he had not actually seen *Ranger* sink as von Bulow was at the periscope and he only had his word for it.

I was amused to find that my opinion of Wendt was shared by the few of his crew who had escaped before the *U 765* took her last plunge. They were particularly disgusted that he, their captain, was the first man over the side when they abandoned ship.

It was evident we had brought the hunt to a successful conclusion just in time, for, in spite of having eliminated *U 765*, the weather reports started up again to our surprise with hardly a break. From the survivors we learnt that they were indeed at the end of their spell of duty and that their relief had been due to take over on the day they were sunk. So, full of enthusiasm, we set out to try and repeat our success. Operations came to a standstill the next day, however, with the advent of a westerly gale and it was not until the 8th May that we were able to renew our pinning-down tactics on the new arrival.

Once again we ran down the bearing obtained by D/F. On this day conditions for the asdic were unusually bad for mid-Atlantic, partly due to the heavy seas which were still running, but chiefly because we found ourselves in waters teeming with shoals of fish and porpoises.

I suppose we were in the middle of the Gulf Stream, but

whatever the reason the asdic 'ping' brought back echoes on almost any bearing and it was exasperating work trying to classify them and discard those which we reckoned were from the fish shoals. Sometimes we were helped by seeing the fish break surface in panic as they fled before some pursuer, or porpoises would be seen on the bearing, hurrying along with their graceful, arching motion.

But towards the end of a maddening day, Campbell in *Aylmer* called us up to say that he was in contact with something more solid than a shoal of fish. He ran in and attacked but could not subsequently find his target again in the difficult conditions. I brought *Bickerton* and *Bligh* over to lend a hand and a careful search put *Bickerton* on to what seemed like the same contact.

From evidence coming up from the asdic it seemed certain we were on to a submarine, very deep and steering a steady course. Here was a chance to repeat our creeping attack and once again I directed *Bligh* until he was stationed astern of the unsuspecting U-boat and gradually overtaking it. Everything seemed set but with the U-boat travelling at about 4 knots it was going to be a long chase if *Bligh* kept down to the 5 knots which was necessary to avoid his propellers being heard and giving warning to the enemy.

In the awkward sea that was running, Jackie Cooper was finding it difficult to keep his ship steering accurately at that slow speed and he suggested an increase of 2 knots. Over-eager for the denouement and to hear the charges thudding out, and tense with anxiety lest the U-boat's captain should wake up to the fact that we were treading on his tail, I did the one thing I should have avoided and gave permission for the increase in speed.

Two things resulted. The extra turbulence in the water caused by *Bligh's* propellers accelerating masked the target and the asdic beam could not penetrate to it. This put *Bickerton* out of contact temporarily until I took her out to one side so as to give the asdic a clear 'view'.

Then, as the moment to fire came and when the order had just been passed, the crew of the U-boat awoke to their danger. As we plotted their movements from the asdic ranges and bearings, they could be seen to make a sharp alteration of course which took their boat outside the lane of depth-charges which was even then sinking down towards it. Not far outside, for there was very little time before the charges started exploding, but enough to be beyond their lethal range which it must be remembered was under thirty feet. I was furious with myself for this error of judgment into which impatience and impetuosity had led me.

Some enormous air bubbles which came up and burst roughly where we thought the U-boat was and on to which a further attack was made by eye, gave us great hopes that in spite of my error the U-boat had been holed and perhaps sunk, particularly as we were unable to regain contact afterwards despite a diligent search. But our hopes were dashed when on the following morning we intercepted the transmission of the usual weather signal.

What the origin of those air bubbles was I never knew but possibly they were from the U-boat's ballast tanks as they were further vented to take it down even deeper.

By now fuel was running low in my ships and as the *Vindex* could not spare us any it was time to return to harbour. It was very satisfactory to have bagged a U-boat on our first operational trip but I relived in my mind again and again the fatal moments when I allowed myself to run short of the patience which is so essential in the hunting of a submerged U-boat.

On arrival at Belfast, our enforced guest, Captain Wendt, was told to get ready to disembark into the care of the army escort awaiting him. For a week or so he had lived in *Bickerton's* wardroom with my officers on equal terms. One of them, as Wendt left to go ashore, courteously wished him good-bye and said that perhaps they might meet one day after the war. Wendt's only reply was, 'In the next war, I sink you!' A braggart to the last, in spite of his incompetence as a U-boat commander, he left a nasty taste.

CHAPTER 13

My Last Kill

THE orders for our role in the invasion of Europe came in
that fat blue volume familiar now to many, entitled Operation 'Neptune'. Except that it managed to break all records
for the number of amendments and corrections received with
it, it had chiefly an academic interest for us.

The Western Approaches Escort Force was not to be part
of the vast landing operation planned, but were assigned
patrol areas off Ushant and the entrance to the English
Channel, through which it was hoped the U-boats from the
French Atlantic ports must pass in the all-out attack expected on the landing and bombarding fleets. First, however,
we had orders to assemble in Moelfre Bay off the coast of
North Wales where we would await the code-word which
meant that Operation 'Neptune' had begun. The 5th
Escort Group arrived there and anchored, being joined
during the day by other groups till quite a sizeable force
was present.

We were all very tense at the thought of what might be in
store for us. We expected a major effort on the part of the
U-boats to break through our patrol lines to get at the enormous target which the invasion fleet represented. Also we
knew that the Germans were now getting to sea their new
Type XXI U-boats, fitted with 'schnorkel' and capable of
very high underwater speeds.

'Schnorkel', or 'Snort' as it came to be known in our
language, was a device to enable the U-boats to run their
diesel engines while remaining submerged. The diesels required large quantities of air when running and so unless an
intake from the atmosphere was available they could not be
used. The Schnorkel consisted of such an intake in the form

of a funnel which could be raised above the surface while the U-boat itself remained below.

With this device the U-boats were able to surmount their greatest weakness in operation, the necessity to surface for considerable periods to recharge the batteries which gave them their motive power when running submerged. Surfaced to charge batteries, the U-boat was liable to be surprised by aircraft and either attacked there and then if it did not dive smartly enough or, in any case, its position, known and marked, could be passed to an anti-submarine ship which was thus able to start a search with confidence and accuracy.

Now, with only the tip of the snort visible, detection by aircraft or ship's radar was almost ruled out and only a very lucky chance would betray them to the eye of an observer in an aircraft.

These new submarines would test our skill to the utmost to hunt down and, armed with the acoustic homing torpedo, they were capable of hitting back hard at their hunters. It was therefore something of an anti-climax when on reaching our patrol area nothing happened. Other groups had a similar experience and it was soon clear that the Germans had been caught completely by surprise and had planned no large-scale drive up Channel.

On the first day out, we were joined by my old friend the *Mourne*, in which I had done one trans-Atlantic convoy trip, and which was still commanded by Lieut.-Commander Holland RNR. Also on her bridge as Yeoman of Signals was Skelton, who had risen from Signalman to Yeoman (Petty-Officer rate) with me in *Hesperus*. There had been no vacancy for him in his new rate in *Hesperus* so I had had to let him go where he could take charge of his own signal staff. I was very happy at this addition to my force for here was no 'new boy' who had to learn the ropes, but a veteran of the Atlantic Battle and well known to me. It was therefore a particularly bitter blow when tragedy overtook her later.

Each escort group was allotted a patrol area, some fifty miles square and, spread in a wide line abreast, with ships one and a half miles apart, swept to and fro and across the area with their asdics. The absence of any action soon made these patrols monotonous in the extreme, while the teeming fish life of the area made searching with the asdic a frustrating and exasperating business. The shoals of fish would each send back an echo, often very like that from a submarine and each had to be examined, plotted and classified before it could be safely discarded and the sweep renewed. Many of them were so deceptive that depth-charges were dropped amongst them and only when the white bellies of floating fish came to the surface was it clear that it had been another false alarm.

Our base, to which we returned from time to time for fresh victuals and fuel, was Plymouth. We were intruders there and were made to feel ourselves nuisances. Our demands for dockyard assistance were invariably questioned and grudgingly granted.

I particularly remember being disgusted at a refusal to supply my ships with the amount of fresh vegetables demanded, being told they were unobtainable—in June in the West Country! On presenting myself at the office of the local Captain (D), responsible for our welfare, to make my protest, I was astonished to be informed by that personage that I must remember there was a war on, that the vast number of men and women based ashore at Plymouth had equal priority with the seagoers for fresh food, etc., etc.!

During this homily my informant had on his desk a large basket of strawberries from which he helped himself from time to time, presumably to illustrate the low priority I enjoyed in the competition for fresh food! These were petty irritations, but they loomed large in our minds at the time and they served to illustrate what a backwater the great port of Plymouth and Devonport had become, with the shifting of the nerve centre of the Atlantic war to Liverpool and its satellite ports.

Another illustration of this was given me when, on visiting the underground headquarters at Plymouth to make my report on a patrol, I happened to meet a very senior officer who asked me how things were going. On explaining the difficulties we were experiencing in the use of asdic in the

Channel owing to the great number of submerged obstruc-
tions, each of which must be carefully investigated in case it
should be a submarine sitting on the sea-bed, this venerable
character nodded. 'Ah yes,' he said, 'but of course you have
your hydrophones to help you.' There was little point in
trying to enlighten him, though hydrophones had not been
used to hunt submarines since the early days of the 1914-18
War!

Fortunately every other time we needed to return to base
for fuel we were allowed to go to our own port of Belfast
where we found people who 'spoke the same language'.

As time went on and the U-boats remained relatively inactive, our patrols were brought further into the Channel. It
was on one of these that we had our first encounter with one
of the new U-boats.

At first light on the morning of 15th June, 1944, a day of
glassy calm and hot blue sky, a report came to me of a patch
of smoke on the surface of the water some miles ahead of us.
It was soon realised that we were probably getting our first
sight of a submarine using its 'schnorkel' and unaware that
the exhaust gases from its diesel motors were leaving a
condensation trail.

The group was quickly re-disposed so as to sweep in a
broad line down on to the position where the smoke was last
seen and I prayed that the glassy calm conditions and the
hot sun would not yet have produced bad asdic conditions
as they undoubtedly would as the day wore on.

The possibility of the U-boat striking back with its acoustic
torpedoes came to my mind as we approached the enemy.
There were two alternative precautions open to me. I could
order all ships to stream their CATS—the noise-makers
towed astern to divert the acoustic torpedoes away from the
propeller noises; or I could order a speed of 7 knots or less,
at which speed it was believed that propeller noises were not
great enough to actuate the homing device in the torpedo.

The noise of the CATS greatly reduced the efficiency of the
asdic, drowning, as it did, any but the loudest echoes. I
would never forgive myself if we missed this golden opportunity for the sake of the extra safety they supplied. So,

'Speed 7 knots,' I ordered, and at this sluggard pace we bore down.

Soon we knew that we must be about in asdic range of the U-boat and excitement became intense. Then came a brief signal from *Mourne*, stationed a mile on my port side. 'Am in contact, Attacking.' It was the last signal that she ever made. Almost simultaneously, a tremendous explosion shook her and *Mourne* literally disintegrated under our eyes. Within a few seconds nothing was to be seen of her but some floating wreckage.

On the bridge of *Bickerton* we were horror-stricken and could not help thinking of our friends whom we had known in the *Mourne*. But there was no time for sorrow. Immediate action was necessary, for to continue steaming on our present course was perhaps to drive right into the remainder of the U-boat's pattern of torpedoes. Quickly the necessary signals were made to turn the flotilla away from the danger area and then to come back from another direction to hunt the U-boat. As we passed the wreckage of *Mourne* on our search we could see survivors clinging to wreckage, but it would have been madness to let a ship stop to pick them up and present herself a sitting target. I had to harden my heart for the time being.

For several hours we searched back and forth for the U-boat but no answering 'ping' came on our asdics. The survivors from *Mourne* were then picked up by the *Aylmer* who took them back to Plymouth, but never another smell did we get of the submarine.

Although I knew that water conditions in that hot, calm sea were against us, I was nevertheless very crestfallen that one of my group could be picked off and not be avenged. Later, when the survivors were questioned, it was evident that *Mourne* had fallen victim to an acoustic torpedo for it was actually seen to pass quite slowly up the *Mourne's* side and suddenly turn in and hit her square in her fore magazine which exploded and tore the ship to pieces.

The galling part of it was that the group had been steaming at the slow speed which makes a ship immune to the homing capabilities of these GNATS, as they were known, but, on gaining contact, Holland had rung down for attacking speed just as the torpedo was passing and missing him. The increased noise from the propellers as the ship accelerated probably attracted the GNAT and disaster occurred.

This tragedy made me realise how these improved U-boats were enabling the enemy to even the balance between hunter and hunted. No more had a well-handled ship the mastery over a U-boat, so long as an efficient antidote to the acoustic torpedo was lacking.

We were a sad and subdued company in *Bickerton* for the rest of that patrol and we were glad when our next was ordered for an area further up Channel between the Cherbourg peninsula and Portland Bill, for the monotony of the first few patrols, broken at length by this tragedy and failure, had sickened us of the Channel Approaches area. We felt our luck might return with a change of scene and we were indeed soon to avenge the *Mourne*.

The U-boats were at last showing some enterprise and had begun to make up-Channel to try to get at the invasion fleet. They had not succeeded in this, but two of them had been sunk by other escort groups, one off the Lizard by the escort group under Ronnie Mills, a term-mate of mine and an old friend, and another by the group commanded by Clive Gwinner. We were prepared, therefore, for a busy time.

We got it, but not at first from direct contact with the enemy. The asdic picked up a plethora of targets, each of which had to be carefully investigated and a decision made as to whether it was a submarine lying on the bottom or a wreck or perhaps a sharp pinnacle of rock sticking up from the sea-bed.

The English Channel has been a busy sea-route for a thousand years and more and in the course of time many hundreds of ships, through stress of weather, or in collision, or in battle have sunk and now lie mouldering on the sea-bed. The asdic faithfully recorded each one of these we came across and the 'ping' of the echo would bring me tumbling out of my sea-cabin to the bridge.

An experienced anti-submarine team, given time to investigate, can fairly reliably distinguish between these false contacts and a moving submarine; but a submarine in shallow waters can settle quietly on the bottom and thereupon becomes, so far as an asdic set can tell, another wreck.

A specialised form of sound apparatus which would record graphically the shape of the object from which the echo was coming was being developed, but at that time it was still in the experimental stage and we were not fitted with it. Sometimes a similar picture of the shape of the object could be obtained by running over it and getting a recording on the echo-sounder of the change of depth as one ran along its length. It was extremely difficult to get directly over the object, however, particularly when one's ship was in the grip of the fierce Channel tides.

Again, one could get a rough idea of the size of the object by the arc over which an echo could be obtained, for from this and the range a simple trigonometrical calculation would give its length. If obviously too big to be a submarine it could be safely disregarded except to make a new mark on the chart to record its position.

This at first was no insurance against the same target being suspected again and again, for navigation out of sight of close landmarks is only accurate within hundreds of yards. To be sure that a contact was an old acquaintance it needed to be accurate within yards. Fairly soon we were very glad to receive the assistance of the marine version of the air navigation device known as 'Gee', which gave us this accuracy and the number of false contacts attacked, or on which time to investigate was wasted, was greatly reduced.

Even so, for twenty-four hours a day it was rare for an hour to pass without the necessity to stop and sniff round a contact and perhaps make an attack because in doubt, or to wait while another ship of the patrol line went through the same process. Some of the wrecks must have been plastered with hundreds of depth-charges and often after an attack pieces of buoyant types of cargo would come bobbing to the surface or a long slick of heavy fuel oil would stream away down-tide to prove that our hoped-for swan was only after all a goose.

Apart from the frustration that these alarms induced, the

constant calls to the bridge, day and night, were immensely wearying for COs and their asdic control officers. However we had our diversions too. The southern end of one of the patrol areas was off the coast of the island of Alderney which, long after much of France had been liberated, still contained a German garrison, who manned some long-range heavy guns. No one had had time to go and mop them up and each time we approached the southern limit of this patrol, these guns would open up at one of the ships of the patrol line.

It was said that they were able to take our range by apparatus which ranged on the heat from our funnels. Whether this was true or not, they were remarkably accurate and, had they been able to fire salvos from several guns at once, they might well have hit us. The chances of a single gun hitting a moving ship were not very good however, and we were not greatly alarmed though we did not linger within range.

On one occasion a carrier-pigeon landed on the deck of *Bickerton* and we felt we were partaking in a real cloak-and-dagger story when it was found to be carrying a message from the French resistance giving details of the location of a German HQ and asking for an air strike. One of the group was sent at full speed into Portland with the message, but I never heard whether the strike was duly 'laid on'.

Perhaps our most exciting side-show took place in dense fog when the *Keats* picked up a radar contact in an area where no surface ship should have been, and set off in chase. Over the radio-telephone we received a moment to moment account of the hunt, culminating in a frenzied shout of 'Submarine in sight', followed, alas, almost immediately by a correction to say that the target was a landing craft.

The landing craft was under the command of a very young officer, well and truly lost in the fog and apparently without charts. He was given a course for his destination and sent happily on his way, while Lieut.-Commander Keene, commanding *Keats*, nursed his bitter disappointment. However, later in the campaign he was to be responsible for sinking two U-boats to make up for it.

As I have said, these constant 'alarums and excursions' were dreadfully wearying and inevitably one got less meticulous in investigating contacts, being predisposed to judge them 'phoney' after so many false alarms. When at last we found an enemy, this nearly robbed me of success.

On the night of 25th June, I had been investigating a contact, which yet again proved to be a wreck, and was steaming at high speed to catch up my group which had carried on the patrol. Exhausted after a long day, I was snatching a few moments of sleep.

Even in my cabin under the bridge, I was never out of earshot of the steady 'Pingggg', 'Pingggg', of the asdic, and an echo coming back would wake me out of the deepest sleep. It did so now. I could hear the officer of the watch setting in motion the investigating procedure and summoning Bill Ridley to the bridge. The echo was extraordinarily loud, far too loud to be from a submarine, I thought, and said so when Bill reported to me down the voice pipe.

Of course, I should have gone at once to the bridge to study the plot as it developed and to harken carefully to the nature of the note coming back on the asdic, but weariness and frustration were taking their toll and I almost was hoping that it would turn out to be just another wreck and I could get back to the sleep which every nerve of my body seemed to be demanding. But the faithful Bill was on the job. He shook me out of my lethargy and insisted that we should not too lightly discard the target we were holding.

I dragged myself to the bridge where the keen night air blew the nonsense out of my brain.

'We have just passed over the target,' Bill told me. 'We should pick her up astern any moment now.' Even as he spoke the answering echo to our 'ping' was heard. The range and bearing was quickly applied at the plotting table and it was at once apparent that the target had moved quite a distance since last plotted. My last doubts vanished. It must be a U-boat.

Quickly I swung the ship's head round, while the alarm rattlers sent all hands to action stations. Now for a steady, careful approach. The submarine could not go deep here in the comparatively shallow waters of the Channel, so shallow depth settings were ordered for the charges. That an acoustic torpedo might have been fired at us crossed my mind, but there was no time to go through the process of streaming our CAT. 'Get in quick and smash him before he knows what is happening' was my plan.

As the range came steadily down and contact remained firm, the moment came to pounce. Ringing down for 20 knots I steered *Bickerton* in to the firing position. As we swept across the U-boat's path, Bill Ridley at the asdic control rapped out the orders 'Fire One!' 'Fire Two!' 'Fire Three!' spacing out the pattern of charges so as to place the target squarely in the centre. With the usual spectacular display of a night depth-charge attack the explosions shook the ship from end to end and almost immediately a U-boat rose like Leviathan out of the sea and lay wallowing.

'Permission to open fire, sir?' yelled the gunnery officer.

'Yes, give them hell,' was my unorthodox reply, and as we swung round in a broad arc to run back to deliver the *coup de grâce*, the night became brilliant with the racing balls of 20mm tracer shells, the flash from our 3-inch guns and the beams of our searchlights. The 3-inch 'Elephant Guns' justi-fied our lack of confidence in them for the shells could be seen to bounce off the submarine's hull without exploding.

As we ran in, however, we could see in our searchlight's beam the crew of the U-boat abandoning ship. Firing ceased and almost at once the submarine turned its bow up into the air and slid stern first to the bottom. *U 269* had gone to join the myriad wrecks littering the floor of the English Channel.

The whole action had taken less than ten minutes, but so packed with intense excitement had they been that as quiet settled down with the guns silent again, I felt as though I had been running a mile race. My first reaction was to slap Bill Ridley's shoulder and congratulate him. 'That one was all yours, Bill,' I cried. 'Yours and your asdic team's. A lovely bit of work and the quickest sinking on record I'll bet.'

'Thank you,' replied Bill. 'That's one in revenge for the *Mourne*.'

The business of picking up the survivors was a fairly

lengthy process. The engineer officer is believed to have gone down with his ship making sure that the sea-cocks were open and that she would not remain on the surface to be captured, and a few of the crew were killed by our gunfire. The remainder were swimming, and scrambling nets were put over the side for them and life rafts launched. Some were wounded and it took time to help them on board. One or two were in very bad shape and, in spite of the efforts of the flotilla doctor, soon died.

On our way back to Plymouth to land our prisoners, the dead were buried at sea and in the presence of their comrades I read the burial service over them before committing them to the sea. I am afraid I found it impossible to refer to them as 'our dear brothers' as in the Prayer Book and I skated round that bit. The bearing and smartness of this U-boat's crew were remarkable, having in mind their recent experience and the shock they must have suffered.

It must by then have been clear to them that Germany had lost the war but their personal morale was quite unshaken.

Interrogation of the officers gave us the answer to the question which had been puzzling us. Why had the U-boat behaved in such a way as to make itself such an easy target? Apparently they had heard the group pass over them while they were lying 'bottomed' as they had heard other patrols do also, and, reckoning that there must be an interval of peace and quiet before another group would come along, they decided to surface or to come to 'schnorkelling' depth for a breath of fresh air.

The propeller noises of *Bickerton* approaching were drowned in those of the rest of the group and by the time the Germans realised we were upon them it was too late to evade our attack. The depth-charges burst all round them and wreaked fearful havoc in the boat so that there was nothing they could do but surface and abandon ship.

While I was away, disaster overtook one of the flotilla. The command had devolved on Jackie Cooper, at this time commanding the *Goodson*. As they patrolled their allotted area in search of further U-boats, *Goodson* was suddenly shaken by a shattering explosion under her stern. Into the air was thrown everything movable on her quarter-deck. Depth-charges, heavy electrical junction boxes, ventilators, crashed down on deck again or into the sea alongside, as the ship heeled over and lay listing to starboard. She had fallen victim to an acoustic torpedo.

The remainder of the Group searched feverishly round *Goodson* with their asdics, trying to locate the U-boat responsible, but in spite of the periscope being sighted at one moment, they achieved no success. Meanwhile in *Goodson* the sea was pouring in at a rate too great for her pumps to cope with and the list was getting worse every moment. Large holes had been torn in the ship's side and bottom plating and the bulkheads of the after-compartments which had to be quickly plugged if the ship was to be saved.

Jackie called for volunteers to dive below the thick and oily water in these spaces, taking down with them wooden plugs, sacking and canvas. Two of his ratings selected from a host of volunteers, an engine-room artificer named Simpson and an Able-Seaman Cribb, went down repeatedly and made such a good job of the temporary repairs that the pumps at last began to beat the inrush of water.

While this was going on *Bligh* was ordered to take *Goodson* in tow. Lieut.-Commander Blyth, her captain, cool and collected in the midst of a very hectic scene, handled his ship superbly and in a very short time the two of them were under way for Portland, where they safely arrived later.

CHAPTER 14

The Biter Bit

BUT our time in the South was nearly up. Back in Belfast in July, we received orders to sail for Scapa Flow to join the Home Fleet in an operation in Arctic waters. This was an assignment I had always dreaded for two reasons. Firstly, the fleet had once before got its hooks on to me, in the winter of 1941, and I knew the utter tedium which it would involve. For inevitably our role would be to screen some big ships usually steaming at too high a speed for my 18-knotters or even my own 24-knot ship for this to be effective. With the small margin of speed available, life would be one long rush at full power to maintain station. Furthermore, our tiny ships could never punch into the weather like the carriers and cruisers we should be screening so that in anything like rough weather we would be suffering weather damage or having to ask for reductions of speed.

Secondly, I knew that the Arctic waters were for long periods the worst possible medium for the sound-waves of the asdic, owing to the severe variations in the water temperature at various depths. Without the asdic these specialised anti-submarine frigates were virtually helpless.

I am probably as little psychic as anyone can be, but a deep sense of foreboding came over me when these orders arrived, which in the event proved to be justified.

However, there was no escape and early in August we sailed. We took that loveliest of all routes around our coasts, up through the Sounds of Jura and Mull, round Skye and up the Minches. In the glorious weather as we steamed north, we made sure of keeping up the reputation of Western Approaches command by painting our ships and generally 'tiddlying up'.

On arrival at Scapa we steamed through the lines of the

Home Fleet destroyers swinging at their buoys in Gutta Sound and I was horrified at the state of dirt and dishevelment they displayed. Their sea-time was probably less than that of most Western Approaches ships and there seemed no excuse for this appalling condition. I can only suppose that lack of action and the general dreariness of their employment when at sea, and of their surroundings when in harbour, had led to a general lowering of tone. Significantly we saw one smart ship as we steamed up the lines, but it wore a foreign ensign!

Having fuelled and secured in our berths, it was clear from information gathered from the HQ ship that the operation for which we had arrived was not due to start for a week or so. Being anxious lest my trained-to-a-hair flotilla should succumb to the sloth and boredom which always prey on an inactive fleet, pulling and sailing regattas and other activities were organised. These were strange activities for wartime but were a great success, particularly as my own ship was soundly beaten, which always gives the junior ships the liveliest satisfaction.

The operation which was impending was twofold. A large-scale air strike by naval aircraft from carriers would be delivered on the *Tirpitz* in Tromso, while simultaneously a convoy for Russia would be rounding the North Cape, the idea being that it would stretch German resources too far for them to take effective action against both. I had hoped that my group might be detailed to join the convoy escort, the only job for which the ships were suitable, but it was not to be.

We were to form the screen for a squadron consisting of the cruiser *Kent* and the escort carriers *Nabob* and *Trumpeter*, and on the 18th August, 1944, we sailed.

On arrival at the area from which the aircraft would be launched, the fleet of which our squadron formed a part proceeded to steam up and down, turning from time to time into wind to fly off or land aircraft.

Every time course was reversed my relatively slow ships had to steam at full power, madly trying to take up their stations ahead and on the bow of the big ships on their new course. By the time this breathless rush was completed, it was about time to repeat the operation all over again. No doubt we formed some slight physical obstruction to a submarine attack so perhaps we fulfilled some useful function.

The fleet continued in the same small sea area for two days and I was surprised that the U-boats known to haunt these waters made no attempt to attack. But the time came for the fleet to withdraw to a refuelling rendezvous to the westward, before renewing the air attacks, and there had been no sign of enemy reaction. Our squadron set off with my group disposed ahead and abeam of them as a screen. The sea was calm, a leaden, sullen, quietly heaving mass under a grey sky. Tests on surface targets with our asdic sets had been giving results which showed that conditions would be bad for detecting submarines.

Relative peace and quiet prevailed as we were on a steady course for a while, except for the normal zigzag, and the wardroom being just below the bridge in the Captain Class frigates, I had felt safe in accepting the invitation of my officers to a game of bridge.

We were in cheerful mood. The passage to the refuelling area should give us a respite from the incessant manœuvring inherent in the operation of carriers flying air strikes off and on. 'I cannot get over the absence of any U-boat activity, with us ploughing up and down the same area,' I remarked. 'Thank heavens for it,' Bill Ridley replied. 'The water conditions for the asdic could not be worse.'

The words were hardly out of his mouth when a dull thump reverberated through the ship. 'That's an underwater explosion,' I cried as I dashed for the ladder to the bridge. As I reached it the officer of the watch was ringing the alarm bells. A glance at the squadron showed that *Nabob* had been torpedoed aft and she lay, stopped, with her stern low in the water.

Kent and *Trumpeter* sheered off and increased speed, steering away from the danger zone. I had to divide my screening force to deal with the situation.

'1st Division alter course 140° to starboard together,' I

signalled. That would take my half of the flotilla back to the aid of the stricken carrier.

'2nd Division form screen on *Kent* and *Trumpeter*.'

'All ships stream CATS.' For it seemed likely that it was an acoustic torpedo which had struck *Nabob* in the stern.

As we steadied on the new course, I asked Bill, who was keeping an eye on activities on the quarter-deck, 'Is that CAT out yet?'

'Just going out, sir,' he replied. As he spoke, the ship was rent by a shattering explosion under her stern.

A column of water shot into the air in the midst of which could be seen depth-charges, slabs of metal and human bodies. The whole length of the ship whipped madly and the siren started to bellow continuously. American warships have, besides the normal siren, a deeper-toned foghorn with a particularly ear-shattering note and *Bickerton*, having been built in the States, was fitted with one of these. It was this instrument of torture which went off and its appalling racket effectually brought all control in the ship to a standstill, since it was impossible to pass an order even by shrieking in a man's ear.

To make confusion worse confounded, the explosion had burst the tank of liquid, stowed right aft, which was part of the apparatus for making white smoke screens. Immediately, the cloud of white smoke was sucked in by the ventilating fans and blown through the ship from end to end. The choking fumes made it impossible to remain anywhere between decks and even on the upper deck it was necessary to keep to the windward side to be able to breathe. While this state of affairs held I was horrified to see that a small body of our younger and 'greener' sailors had panicked and lowered a whaler into which they proceeded to tumble. Unable to make myself heard or understood while the foghorn continued to roar, I rushed down to the upper deck and managed by gesture and mime to stop the panic and get the boat back alongside. It was a gang of very sheepish and shamefaced men who scrambled back on board.

The sudden cessation of noise as someone in the engine-room staff found the right valve and shut off steam to the siren was a blissful relief. I continued aft to survey the damage and, passing some hideously shattered corpses and burnt and wounded men, I found that the stern had more or less disintegrated. The ship lay with the remains of her stern under water and a heavy list.

It was clear that she could never steam again, but if she was still sound forward there might be a chance of towing her home. It was essential, therefore, for an examination between decks to be made, a job calling for considerable nerve in a ship obviously badly damaged, lying low in the water and with the sluggish, crank roll which indicated lost stability. I knew that she might sink very suddenly should a major bulkhead give way. I was pleased, therefore, after the poor showing by some of the ship's company, that there was no difficulty in getting volunteers. A party led by Stoker Petty-Officer Taylor, with P.O. Winter, Ordnance Mechanic Chapman and A.B. Steele, hurried off and soon came back with the surprising news that although most of the stern and quarter-deck were missing, the remainder of the ship from the after engine-room bulkhead was as sound as a bell. Once again one of these splendid little ships had shown their amazing capacity to take punishment and survive.

Whether it would be possible to get her home or not, the first essential was to get the wounded and the non-essential members of the ship's company out of the ship and into one of our consorts. It seemed only too likely that the U-boat would be back to finish off its half-completed job on both *Bickerton* and *Nabob*. Now that the first panic had subsided amongst the excitable minority, a panic perhaps excusable when one remembers that at that stage of the war ships' companies had a large proportion of conscripts at sea for the first time in their lives, the evacuation took place in orderly fashion. Indeed, many of the ship's company seemed to go out of their way to set good examples to the doubtful characters, insisting on giving up their places in the queue, joking and wisecracking to raise morale.

The Chief Petty Officer Telegraphist, Brooks, a pensioner and the 'Father' of the ship's company, refused to be hustled and made a great show of methodically arranging for disposal of code books, etc., which had a steadying effect. A Leading Seaman Rendle and an Electrical Artificer Robinson both set good examples, I remember, while it was heartening to see one man, a stoker named Eyres, with a nasty wound in his head, steadfastly refusing to leave the ship until it was clear that he was the last of the advance party and that he was not doing anyone else out of a place in the boats.

It was a relief when the last of them was gone and safely embarked in *Kempthorne*. Then, if the U-boat should come back for the kill there would be only a few of us to be picked up. Meanwhile a muster of survivors revealed a tragic tale of more than forty men killed. The problem now arose as to what to do for the wounded *Bickerton*. We were in enemy waters, close off the Norwegian coast, but even so if we had had only our own flotilla to think of, one of the others could have taken us in tow with a very good chance of safely making harbour. But we were responsible for providing escort for the *Nabob* where heroic endeavours were being made to repair her damage and get under way.

When her captain (Captain H. N. Lay RCN) reported that he would be able to steam again given a few hours, I realised that the poor *Bickerton* must be regarded as expendable in order to give protection to the much more important escort carrier. Signalling to the C-in-C, I got permission for a destroyer to be detailed to put a torpedo into *Bickerton*, while I transferred to the *Aylmer* with my staff. It was a sad sight to see the gallant little *Bickerton* throw her bows up into the air and slide quickly under the surface.

In the few months that I had commanded her I had become very fond of this mass-produced tin-can of a ship. She could never be the aristocrat that *Hesperus* was, or the faithful old war-horse like *Walker*, but she had shown that she could 'take it' and 'hand it out' as well as either of them.

Meanwhile in *Nabob*, Captain Lay had also taken the precaution to transfer all but essential personnel to ships of the escort group and for the next three hours, while we awaited the seemingly inevitable return of the U-boat to deliver the *coup de grâce*, the flotilla circled the carrier to give what anti-submarine protection we could. That this was not very reliable owing to the water conditions we knew only too well.

At one time in *Bligh* a look-out claimed to have sighted the U-boat momentarily breaking surface but *Bligh* and *Aylmer* could gain no asdic contact. We felt singularly helpless under such conditions but it seems that the U-boat's captain had used up his stock of courage for the day and at last at 2230 that night *Nabob* started to move through the water again—a mere 6 knots at first, but steadily increasing until she was making 10, which she was able to maintain until she got safely into harbour.

The U-boat which had scored this half-success, *U 354*, and which, with a little more resolution could have had the satisfaction of sinking an escort carrier, did not survive to celebrate. Caught on the surface by a Swordfish from our old friend *Vindex*, *U 354* was sent to the bottom a few days later.

On arrival back in Liverpool in *Aylmer*, I found that my sea-going days were over for the time being. Perhaps the C-in-C felt that my luck was beginning to run out at last and that it was time to 'change the bowling'. Certainly I was ready for a rest and I knew from previous experience that it is unwise to ignore the danger signals which warn the tired commander.

I was therefore content to hand over the 5th Escort Group to Commander Bertram Taylor and join my wife and son on leave in Derbyshire. Security being what it was in those days, my wife had no idea that at last her fears had been fulfilled and that I had intercepted a torpedo. It was perhaps a rather abrupt way of finding out when, in answer to her question as to where my luggage might be, I had to admit that my entire stock of clothes was on my back.

Shock and relief seemed to share in her expression about equally and the startling effect of the news on her made me realise for the first time the long-drawn-out suspense she must have been suffering during those years I had been at sea, broken only by the brief hectic days of leave between convoys. I wonder how most men would behave if the roles were reversed—as indeed I suppose they often were in those days of total war.

And so my fighting days came to an end. I confess I was ready for this. Although the Battle of the Atlantic had been virtually won in May, 1943, and our transatlantic convoys had been rarely molested after that time, the invasion of Europe coupled with the German production of the 'Schnorkel' submarine had opened a new phase in the war against U-boats. Fought largely in the shallow waters around our coasts, with the air thick with our aircraft and the odds greatly in our favour, it was yet in many ways a more wearying fight than those in defence of our convoys. More wearying, of course, for both sides. For the U-boats there can have been only brief periods when they were not in sight or sound of our hunting forces and, though the detection of a submerged U-boat amongst the shoals and wrecks was of extreme difficulty, the possibility was continuously with them and once detected in shallow water their end was certain.

The hunters, on the other hand, knew no peace night or day, fair weather or foul, on clear days or in deepest fog. Everlastingly the asdic picked up echoes from rocks, from tide rips, shoals of fish, from wrecks and each time only painstaking check and recheck could differentiate these contacts from that of a U-boat. And while the ships nosed the scent and decided whether to go in for the kill, a deadly acoustic torpedo might be homing on to the sound of their propellers.

Under these conditions we all became quickly very, very tired. Lack of sleep was, of course, one factor, but another was the knowledge that for sixty minutes every hour and for twenty-four hours of every day there was never a moment that might not bring that shattering concussion of an exploding torpedo. Freshness and a never-wearying alertness were essential to come out on top in this game and I knew I was losing them. It was time for me to go.

CHAPTER 15

The Future

THE Second World War, like the First, came perilously near to being lost on the ocean trade routes. The Navy's role from time immemorial has been the defence of our trade and to ensure the free movement of our ships so that not only can food and munitions of war, a great deal of which must be imported, be brought in, but so that we are free to strike our land-based enemy at any point of our choosing on his coasts.

It is often claimed that the advent of weapons of mass destruction, such as the hydrogen bomb, has entirely altered the Navy's role. Indeed, extremists go so far as to say that navies are no longer of practical use in a major war. Preparing for a war at sea, they say, is making the old mistake of preparing for the last war. What is the use of making plans for the protection of our supplies by sea when this country will be nothing but a smoking ruin?

But will war, when it comes, be opened by a brisk exchange of these ghastly weapons? What man will have the temerity to give the order which will mean the end of civilisation on Earth? Certainly no British Prime Minister, for this country is the most vulnerable of any in the world to weapons of mass destruction. An American President? Perhaps today, when the USA is to a great extent immune from retaliation. But with the development of Polar flight and long-range rockets capable of carrying hydrogen bombs, what then? And if the Russians are preparing to launch an atomic war, why then are they building up a first-class navy, including some 400 ocean-going submarines?

If we really believe that war inevitably means an atomic war, then let us have the courage of our beliefs, abolish the Royal Navy, and devote all our efforts to maintaining an

Air Force at instant readiness to deliver a knock-out blow before we ourselves are wiped out.

But I do not think our rulers do believe this. Surely a world war is more likely to develop from small beginnings, such as a Middle East skirmish, into which the great powers would be drawn in on account of alliances, treaties of friendship or guarantees of frontiers. While the fearful decision whether or not to use the hydrogen bomb in such a war was being made, this country might well be starving as a result of an all-out submarine attack on our shipping. For with the escort forces at present at our disposal there is no need for an enemy to use the hydrogen bomb to defeat us.

What does seem certain to me is that the half-and-half measures we are taking are useless whichever form of war should come: we are maintaining a fleet which is too weak to fulfil its functions in an orthodox war and which is valueless to us if we become the target for hydrogen bombs.

When fleets all sailed on the surface of the sea, victory was ensured by seeking out the enemy's surface fleet and bringing it to battle. With the invention of the submarine this no longer sufficed. With only a token enemy surface fleet, a bold and ruthless submarine campaign could, and nearly did, bring us to our knees. The enemy we had to bring to battle was the U-boat fleet, and we found that the only way to do this was to put our merchant ships into escorted convoys so that if he was to achieve anything he must accept encounter with our warships. To hunt the U-boat in the wide spaces of the ocean was conclusively proved to be a waste of time unless and until we had such enormous forces on the sea and in the air that we could saturate the whole area. It took four years of frantic shipbuilding and aircraft manufacture by the two greatest industrial nations of the time to achieve these numbers, though we started the Second World War with a much larger fleet of ships suitable for escort than we are likely to another time.

And the U-boats against us then were mere 'submersibles', ships which could submerge for comparatively short periods of time but must surface to charge batteries and renew the air, or if they wished to move at more than 4 knots or so— a fast walking pace. The submarines of today are mostly at an intermediate stage between the submersible and the true submarine for they still depend on an intake of air to keep going but they need not completely surface to obtain it. It is the submarine of tomorrow, however, that we must consider. This will be able to do over 25 knots submerged and it will not need to surface at all during its entire cruise. It will be armed with torpedoes of far greater efficiency which will be able to 'home' on to their targets in a manner similar to the acoustic torpedoes used by the Germans and with others which can be pre-set to zigzag across the target's course as were the German 'Lut' torpedoes.

How are such submarines to be detected, hunted and destroyed? No matter how thickly we can space our air or surface searches over the sea, unless submarines put some portion of themselves, such as a 'snort', above the surface they will be able to proceed indefinitely undetected. But one thing is certain; if they are to achieve their object they must eventually arrive in a small area in the vicinity of their target. So once again we come back to the same solution, namely to concentrate the target as much as possible, i.e., in convoys, and to mass our anti-submarine forces around the convoys. Thus by action of an apparently defensive nature we take the offensive. We bring the enemy to battle. It may perhaps seem that by this system we are using our merchant ships as 'bait', but this is far from the case. It is the independently routed ship that is in far greater danger.

During the Second World War from the time that our escorting forces became reasonably efficient and well-equipped, the strategy of the German U-boat command made this crystal clear. The Germans avoided attacking convoys if they could, first by cruising ever further westward so as to catch our ships after the escorts had left and the convoys dispersed; then on America's entry into the war the U-boats left the convoy route and concentrated gleefully on the US coast where ships sailed independently. Only when this 'happy time' came to an end did they once again challenge the escort forces of the Western Approaches and they took such a hiding that Admiral Dönitz was forced to admit defeat and withdraw them altogether from the North Atlantic.

Throughout the war only a small minority of ships sailed independently and they were nearly all fast ships. Yet of all ships lost at sea by enemy action 72 per cent were sailing alone.

Perhaps at this point any idea that in the foreseeable future our trade can be carried by aircraft should be dispelled. The largest aircraft of today can carry perhaps 20 tons of cargo. Five hundred of these aircraft, each costing some million pounds today, and manned by at least 3,000 highly-skilled personnel, would be required to carry the cargo of one typical freighter. Something like 125 such ships every week were coming into our ports during the last war to keep us supplied. Furthermore, before such a gigantic air-lift can function, the fuel for the aircraft will have to be imported by sea in any case. No! It will be a very long time before even a fraction of our vital supplies can be brought in by air.

If it is agreed that our ships must sail in escorted convoys, however, the question then arises as to the nature of the escort. It is, of course, axiomatic that aircraft of one sort or another must form part, perhaps the major part, of the escort in future. During the last war, out of 2,353 ships sunk by the enemy, only 19 were lost from convoys which had a combined surface and air escort. Controversy arises, however, over where these aircraft are to come from and who should control them. One school of thought believes that shore-based aircraft can provide all the air support that is necessary and even goes so far as to say that a shore-based air force can control the whole war at sea. Having seen how long it took in the last war to achieve even a moderate degree of understanding by shore-based airmen of the problems involved in the defence of a convoy, I am convinced that such ideas are the wildest nonsense.

A shore-based airman arriving over a convoy at sea (and we hope that this initial step to bring support will be more reliably achieved than in the past) cannot be in possession of all the minute-to-minute information and intelligence which is essential to its defence. The information essential to him, and the instructions as to what is required of him, must be transmitted to him by the escort commander—no easy task in foul weather and never a quick one, with perhaps radio silence in force, or if, as so often happens, radio communication fails. An airman whose base is in a ship, either in the convoy or in its vicinity can be in action, or starting his patrol, within minutes of being briefed. Furthermore, he will be a trained expert in air/sea co-operation and not, like his shore-based equivalent, temporarily carrying out a tiresome variation of his normal flying duties. The naval aviator will be part of a team, trained together. The shore-based man will be a stranger brought in at the last moment and not altogether sure of the rules.

I am convinced, therefore, that, as we learnt in the war, a convoy must carry its own air escort with it. Today this means aircraft carriers of one sort or another, although with the development of helicopters these may no longer be necessary. The answer to the submarine with the high submerged speed must be aircraft capable of searching for and detecting it fully submerged. For small surface ships, in anything but moderate seas, are restricted in their speed and the modern submarine can outpace them by remaining submerged and making up wind. Helicopters would seem, therefore, to be the most fruitful line of development.

But a close escort of warships is still as necessary as ever. The process of shepherding a convoy is a continuous one which goes on night and day from the time of sailing until it reaches its destination. All the multifarious actions necessary to ensure its 'safe and timely arrival' can only be undertaken by the man on the spot, the escort commander, who must have authority over all the forces forming the escort whether ships or aircraft. To allow inter-service jealousy to bedevil such basic principles is to my mind criminal lunacy. Unfortunately the protagonists of the air age have always had the backing of those who, with little or no knowledge of the sea, like to be thought 'forward thinkers'. Many of our popular newspapers are among them and if, should the challenge come again, we were to find that in deference to the 'forward thinkers' the Navy had been allowed to dwindle, in the belief that in this air age only shore-based aircraft are needed to defend our trade, then people of this island would be in for a very rude shock.

In 1939 we had in reserve more than seventy destroyers built towards the end of the First World War and still in a good state of repair. They gave wonderful service and many of them were still in commission at the end of the war. What we should have done without them in 1940 and 1941 I shudder to think. Destroyers built during the last war were, however, for reasons of economy, built of ungalvanised 'black' steel, and the majority have long since rotted away and been scrapped or placed on the disposal list. Moreover, only a pitiful number of new frigates and escort vessels are coming forward to replace them. Money is not allocated to provide for these apparently 'defensive' weapons, while it is lavished on 'offensive' bombers. But as I have said before, convoy escort is essentially offensive. It enables us to bring the enemy fleet to battle as nothing else can.

Before 1918, the taxpayer had two fighting services only to pay for. The simplicity of the weapons of that time kept the cost of upkeep of a large navy and a small army down to a level that could well be borne by the prosperous country that we then were.

The formation of the Royal Air Force at the end of the First World War added a third burden to the defence vote, with all the added overheads of a separate ministry and separate supply organisation. This was no doubt inevitable and wise, but from the taxpayer's point of view it means a third greedy hand held out once a year for a share in the nation's income. The politicians who decide how much each service should get are but human. They are swayed in their decisions by propaganda of various sorts; the more intelligent no doubt chiefly by any books on strategy they may read; others, and probably the majority, by views expressed in the popular Press, which is usually entirely superficial in its outlook. Air power and the wonders of the Air Age are dramatic and colourful. Every small boy knows all about the latest jet fighter or H-bomber. But the unspectacular business of defending our merchant shipping, so vital to our survival in war, has little or no news value or glamour and until we get near to disaster is largely pushed out of sight and out of mind.

There are few objections raised, therefore, to the provision of funds for our Air Force. Our aircraft can be seen and heard, day and night, weaving their trails in the sky, and the tax-payer can see his money being put to use. But he is reluctant to put his hand in his pocket to pay for a navy which is only seen when in harbour and of whose function he knows little or nothing. It is only too understandable, this lack of appreciation of the meaning and value of sea-power. After all, Napoleon never understood it to his dying day, though it was sea-power which brought him to his ruin. Hitler, too, placed his faith in armies and air-power, but it was sea-power again that brought his triumphal progress to a halt in 1940.

Throughout our history we have neglected our navy in times of peace, but probably never to the disastrous degree we are doing so now. To defeat the German U-boat campaign in the last war we were forced to send to sea many hundreds of anti-submarine vessels of all sorts, as well as a great number of escort aircraft carriers. Today, faced by the enormous Russian submarine fleet, we have no escort carriers and only a handful of escort vessels.

A navy is not a thing that can be quickly built up. Admittedly, small warships can be built a great deal more quickly today than of old, but they are of little value without the trained and disciplined men to sail them. The experience of the Canadian Navy in the war, which I have mentioned earlier, makes this abundantly clear. A well-found and armed warship with an untrained and inexperienced crew is as bad as no ship at all. Indeed, it may be a positive menace—for it will fail us when we are relying upon it to fulfil some vital task.

Today our sea-going navy is so small that many a man spends year after year in the service without ever getting to sea. For officers the situation is just as bad: young Commanders, with a brilliant sea-going career behind them, are informed that they are on the 'dry' list and will never go to sea again, because of the shortage of ships. Electronics, guided missiles, atomic power—none of these affect the necessity for seamanship and the understanding of the 'way of a ship in the midst of the sea'. A ship is such a puny thing in the grip of the fury of the elements at sea. To keep afloat, let alone to fight a ship, under these conditions, takes knowledge and experience that cannot be learnt in lecture-rooms.

Let us hope, therefore, that this great maritime nation may once again come to realise that in spite of hydrogen bombs, in spite of the wonders of supersonic flight and atomic energy, our lifeblood still flows along the ocean trade-routes and that the primary necessity is to protect that bloodstream with an efficient and adequate navy.